Y0-CBX-864

HUMAN/NATURE

HUMAN/

NATURE

Biology, Culture, and

Environmental History

EDITED BY

John P. Herron

& Andrew G. Kirk

WITH A

FOREWORD BY

Carolyn Merchant

University of

New Mexico Press

Albuquerque

© *1999 by the University of New Mexico Press*
All rights reserved.

FIRST EDITION

Library of Congress Cataloging-in-Publication Data
Human/nature : biology, culture, and environmental
history / edited by John P. Herron & Andrew G.
Kirk ; with a foreword by Carolyn Merchant. — 1st
ed.

p. cm.

Based on papers from the New Mexico
Environmental Symposium held in Albuquerque,
April 1996.

Includes bibliographical references.

ISBN 0-8263-1916-5 (paper)

ISBN 0-8263-1915-7 (cloth)

1. Human beings — Effect of environment on —
Congresses. 2. Human ecology — Congresses.
3. Nature and nuture — Congresses.
4. Sociobiology — Congresses. 5. Philosophy
of nature — Congresses. I. Herron, John P.,
1968– . II. Kirk, Andrew G., 1964– .
III. New Mexico Environmental Symposium
(1996 : Albuquerque, N.M.)

GF51.H76 1999

304.2 — dc21   98-48696

CIP

CONTENTS

Part II   /   Human/Nature Stories

ACKNOWLEDGMENTS

This volume had its origins in a conference, the New Mexico Environmental Symposium (NMES), held in Albuquerque in April 1996. Major funding for the conference came from the New Mexico Endowment for the Humanities. Under the direction of John Lucas, the NMEH provided significant financial support crucial to the success of the event. In addition, University of New Mexico provost William Gordon, through the College of Arts and Sciences, also engineered a substantial grant during the midst of a serious budget crisis. His commitment to the project demonstrated a willingness to place education above bureaucracy. The UNM Graduate and Professional Student Association provided much needed travel funds and support, as did the History Graduate Student Association with the help of the outstanding staff of the "Grotto." The UNM history department, first under Jonathan Porter and then Rob Robins, also generously contributed travel funds and administrative support. History department administrator Yolanda Martinez guided us through the mind-boggling wilderness of university accounting and helped cut red tape, saving us days of work. The always gracious Lisa Weatherman helped arrange accommodations and organize conference events. Finally Molly Davis generously donated her valuable time, expertise, and impressive Rolodex to help market the conference.

In addition to financial support many individuals volunteered their time, ideas, and energy for this project. Matthew Powell, Michael Anne Sullivan, Scott Hughes, Dedra McDonald, Rex Renk, and Jerry Davis all provided fantastic introductions for participants and worked at conference events. Another early adviser and supporter was Professor Richard Etulain, whose sage advice on funding, organization, and publication of conference essays proved invaluable as usual. Professor Betsy Jameson also provided introductions, conference advice, support, and goodwill. We also owe a special debt to Hal Rothman. Hal accepted the challenging role of commentator for the conference and delivered the concluding remarks at the close of the main event. His energy enlivened our discussions and contributed greatly to the atmosphere and success of the NMES. Another significant contributor to the conference and this volume was Carolyn Merchant. Although not an official participant, her enthusiastic involvement in the conference, insightful forward to this book, and perceptive comments on the role of human nature in environmental history expanded the depth and complexity of our debate at every stage. One of the strongest supporters of this project from the very beginning was our friend and colleague Timothy Moy. Tim moderated the roundtable at the conference and contributed the superb afterword to this volume. More than anyone involved, he attempted to place our debate within the context of ongoing developments in the sciences and humanities. His consistently even-handed analysis and penetrating critiques provided an admirable model for academic discourse that impressed all who had the pleasure of working with him. Finally Peter Swift, Rebecca Ulrich, Abbe Karmen, Tom Gentry, and members of the human nature reading group provided a friendly and open forum for developing ideas about the subject of this book. Peter Swift in particular, a geologist by trade, contributed a unique perspective and consistently pragmatic grounding for our far-ranging, and sometimes far-out, debates.

Of course the ultimate measure of a conference is the quality of its participants. We were fortunate to recruit a wonderful group of scholars for this project. The willingness of each of these busy people to rearrange their schedules to accommodate two graduate students was amazing and deeply gratifying. The excitement that our idea generated far surpassed our wildest expectations, and the entire experience was a highlight for us both. Another pleasant surprise was the early and strong support from the University of New Mexico Press. Larry Durwood Ball, our editor at UNM Press, became one of the most steadfast supporters of this project. From our earliest meetings at the Frontier, he displayed a remarkable faith in the concept and our ability to bring it to fruition. For over three years Durwood shepherded this project through the publication process and never wavered in his belief that it was a worthwhile exercise. Also invaluable during the publication process were the comments from an anonymous peer reviewer. These particularly incisive observations offered excellent suggestions for revision that contributed greatly to the shape and content of the final manuscript.

The experience of organizing the New Mexico Environmental Symposium and editing this volume was a rare opportunity for two young scholars. We are grateful to everyone who made it possible.

FOREWORD

Carolyn Merchant

Chaco Canyon, San Juan watershed, Anasazi culture, present state of New Mexico, A.D. 1150. Four-story pueblos, thirteen great houses, a multitude of surrounding villages, all constructed of adobe and wood, are set at the base of a canyon. Fields of flourishing vegetables are watered by a vast system of gates and irrigation canals. A system of straight thirty-foot-wide highways stretches out of the canyon, joining adjacent and faraway communities to the central city. On nearby Fajada Butte an observatory measures the timing of the solstices and equinoxes; a shaft of sunlight striking between stone slabs sets planting, harvesting, and festival times for the city's health and security.

Albuquerque, Rio Grande watershed, North American culture, present state of New Mexico, A.D. 1996. Four-story buildings, great houses, skyscrapers, a multitude of suburbs, all constructed of adobe, wood, concrete, and steel, stretch out along the Rio Grande valley. Fields of crops are watered by a vast irrigation system, and a network of roads and highways links the city to surrounding communities. At nearby Los Alamos National Laboratory research on nuclear weapons sets the agenda for the country's defense and security.

Two cities, two watersheds, two human cultures. Striking similarities, vast differences. How to account for them? Nature and human nature both play significant roles in the transformation of a desert landscape into a thriving civilization. The constraints and opportunities imposed by limited

water, vast temperature ranges, a relatively restricted growing season, river
and mesa topography, and clay and sandy soils set many of the options for
human life. Human ingenuity, dexterity, curiosity, communication, and reproductive capacities open opportunities for community living. Nature and human nature interact in the production of human societies. Both are complicated, historically changing, culturally constructed terms. In April 1996 a
group of environmental historians, philosophers, and scholars from related
fields gathered at the University of New Mexico in Albuquerque to focus their
attention on the interconnections between nature and human nature, with
special attention to the underinterrogated meanings of human nature. Their
reflections are reproduced in this volume.

Human nature, like nature itself, is one of the most complex concepts in
western culture. Are there essential traits common to all humans merely by
"nature" of being human? If so, what are they? Are human characteristics a
product of culture, rather than nature, and therefore variable and relative to
particular cultures? Joining the term human to the term nature raises further
questions. Are humans a part of or apart from nature? Is nature one thing and
humans another, or does joining the two mean that humans share something
with nature, whatever that may be? On the other hand, if humans are distinct
from nature, how does human nature differ from nonhuman nature?

All humans seem to share some species-specific "natural" characteristics —
large brains, opposed thumbs, bipedalism, language ability, sexual receptivity,
consciousness, and so on. More problematic are "human" characteristics such
as capacities for love, hate, cooperation, competition, selfishness, altruism,
morality, and so forth. Even more complex and problematic are so called
gender-specific characteristics, such as tendencies to be aggressive, gentle, rational, emotional, giving, protective, adventurous, etc. Are there any "essential" male or female characteristics, and if so, what are they? If such characteristics are not gender-specific, are they culturally assigned and reinforced?
Similar problems and concerns can be raised about characteristics of race and
ethnicity.

Questions such as these are usually not addressed very specifically by writers about nature, culture, gender, or history. Yet assumptions about the answers to these questions underlie each writer's narrative. The ways writers use
adjectives, adverbs, verbs, and nouns imply culturally constructed positions in
relation to these unarticulated questions. The actors and plots they choose to
include or omit reflect underlying assumptions about both nature and human
nature. By asking questions about and attempting to articulate each author's
concept of nature, human nature, theory of history, and prophetic trajectory,

readers can discern much about our unexpressed ideas, politics, hopes, and fears.

Most authors would perhaps agree that there is a biological component to every human being over which layers of a particular culture or cultures are woven. Human biological material seems extraordinarily malleable, although not infinitely so. Humans may be genetically programmed, yet culturally shaped. But is biology or culture more significant in influencing the outcome? For some writers, biological drivers such as the need to satisfy hunger and sex, through production and reproduction, are uppermost in influencing, although not necessarily determining, history. For others, people and history are driven by storytelling, or moral characteristics and imperatives. For still others, there is an inseparable mixture of biocultural factors. Brain and body evolve together. People are biosocial beings. They weave together the warp of culture with the woof of nature.

The contributors to *Human/Nature* have thought hard about these questions and interconnections. They have approached the issues from a variety of social, gender, and racial perspectives. For Paul Hirt, humans are three species in one: *Homo activists* who move, eat, sleep, and reproduce; *Homo economicus,* which represents the social aggregate necessary to satisfy basic human needs and ideals; and *Homo narratus,* or storytellers who justify and rationalize ways of being in the world. For Max Oelschlaeger, humans are culture lovers — overdetermined culturally and underdetermined biologically. They are *sapiens, economicus,* and rational architects who weave stories together as texts. Vera Norwood sees nature as an unmediated flux, with humans interacting with different aspects of it. Women and men are embodied differently; to be incorporated in a different body is to live in a different world.

Virginia Scharff characterizes people as metamorphic, interconnected, moving beings — incomplete puzzles who are products of tools and tool uses. Since the Enlightenment, people must struggle for the privilege of being human; culture affects access to the status of "human being." Andrew Kirk sees people as contingent, historical beings who are masters of their own destiny. For John Herron, they invent social, narrative frameworks that are not wholly in tune with the natural world.

Dan Flores emphasizes the biological side of human nature. Reproduction, sex, and gender exemplify the selfish gene set in a Darwinian context of competition and cooperation. The human animal is a reproducing organism who cannot completely control the widespread implications of its own population explosion. Environmental historians, he believes, need to address the fact that humans have an animal nature by writing through a bioregional lens over the *longue durée.* Tim Moy agrees that sociobiology reveals human nature, but to say that humans are biologically based is a trivial statement. People are biologically shaped, but flexibility is also hard-wired into our biology. Nature, the land, and gender, like human nature, are all problematically constructed concepts, but nevertheless all have great agency in environmental history.

William deBuys views people as the children of culture, whose genetically determined impulses are awakened and overcome by cultural stories. As *Homo narratus,* we invent and reinvent our own core stories that reflect the mix between biology and culture. The stories told by environmental historians fall into three modes — tragic, consensus building, and complex/self-reflective forms of narration.

The flexibility of human biology and ingenuity — the "contriving brain and the skillful hand" — and the narrating capacities of human communication seem to have promoted adaptation to a multitude of varying environments. Environmental historians have played a major role in understanding the implications of those adaptations and their limitations over time. Yet even the narrating abilities of historians cannot predict historical outcomes. Chaco Canyon and Albuquerque, New Mexico, linked together by nature and human nature yet separated in time and human culture, may or may not meet the same fate. By A.D. 1200 only the wind whistled through the abandoned homes of the Chaco peoples. The future of Albuquerque is as yet an open question.

HUMAN/NATURE

INTRODUCTION

Andrew Kirk and John Herron

Human nature is a dead idea. Efforts to uncover a fundamental biological component to human behavior are based on an unsophisticated understanding of both culture and science and contribute little to our exploration of human society. This is an assertion that many scholars would readily agree with, but is it true? Do ideas of human nature no longer play a role in our analysis and understanding of human relations with each other and the environment? Do all scholars really agree that the concept of human nature should finally be put to rest? The basic premise of this volume is that notions of human nature are still very much alive and well and continue to inform and shape our understandings of environmental issues and direct our environmental politics. Some of the uses of human nature are subtle, some are not, but as we approach the new millennium it is a propitious time to reevaluate this central idea from a new perspective.

It is hard to peruse much of the now vast literature of environmental history and politics without encountering implicit or explicit references to the biological basis for human behavior. Many environmental narratives include arguments that find much of their evidence in appeals to universal inherited characteristics. For example, Native Americans venerate the environment, Europeans commodify it, women nurture the earth, men exploit it, enlightened people play in the wilderness, ignorant people work in it.

These illustrations may be extreme, but in some form these dichotomies run throughout most environmental writing. There is little debate that ideas about human nature, from evolution to sociobiology, profoundly influence the shape of current environmental ideas and scholarship.

Appeals to human nature have long served to explain our differences, justify inequalities, categorize similarities, and clarify our behavior. In fact, the belief in a fundamental human nature is one of the central, and most controversial, dogmas of western thought. Yet unlike "nature" and "culture," concepts that have figured centrally in environmental history debates in recent years, human nature has received little attention from environmental scholars. The essays in this book attempt to rectify this omission by critically examining the idea of human nature and its place in environmental discourse and environmental history. Specifically, the authors investigate how ideas about human nature influence the way people think and write about the nonhuman world.

Many popular ideas about the environment and modern environmental problems are premised on the notion that human behavior is, at least to a certain degree, biologically determined. Environmental scholars place varying degrees of emphasis on the biological component to human behavior, from rigid biological determinism to subtle and fluid evolutionary ecology. These perceptions profoundly influence how we see human relationships with the nonhuman world and how we structure our environmental politics. In order to understand how environmental philosophies intersect with and shape our understanding of biological frameworks, a principal concern of environmental history, we must first uncover the underlying assumptions of human behavior that influence that interaction.

The essays in this book explore these questions primarily within the context of environmental history. Originally we intended our investigation of the idea of human nature to serve merely as a starting point for a larger discussion of the intersections between social and environmental history. As we read through the literature of environmental history and environmental politics, however, the complex interaction between ideas about human nature and popular conceptions about human relations with the nonhuman world kept reappearing as a central theme. The literature of environmentalism and environmental history is replete with assumptions about universal human attributes. As several of the essays in this book illustrate, conceptions of human nature are implicit in most environmental writing and explicit in certain genres such as ecofeminism.[1] Most humanists agree that culture and environment shape human behavior at least as profoundly as biology; however, the persistence of inchoate essentialism in the social sciences and humanities suggests that, to paraphrase James Clifford, "human nature" is a deeply compromised idea we cannot yet do without.[2] The very vagueness of the term, the myriad and often contradictory ways it is used, testify to its perplexing but persistent power.

In an effort to understand the complicated social, cultural, political, and historical implications of the idea of human nature, we organized a conference. In the spring of 1996, a diverse group of environmental scholars gathered in Albuquerque to participate in the New Mexico Environmental Symposium. Our goal in organizing this meeting was not to create a consensus on the idea of human nature or to validate the current popular resurgence of this controversial notion. Rather, it was to make visible the idea of human nature and to examine the way it operates in environmentalism and environmental history as an epistemological foundation, a linguistic trope, and a political tool.[3]

This is not to suggest that before this exercise, or now, we thought that environmental historians as a group are unsophisticated in their treatment of the thorny concept of human nature. On the contrary, environmental historians tend to present some of the most nuanced analyses of human and natural history.[4] Environmental historians have led the way in the effort to historicize problematic terms like "nature" and "culture," "civilization" and "wilderness," providing us with a deeper understanding of how ideas are products of particular cultural perceptions and historical circumstances and how culture influences biological relationships.[5] Most convincingly, recent analysis of environmental rhetoric has demonstrated that when people talk about natural relationships and biological determinants, they often reveal more about human history and politics than they intend. Despite these efforts aimed at understanding language and environmental perception, the idea of human nature remains largely unexplored in the context of environmental discourse.

Echoing the sentiments of many environmental scholars, historian William Cronon recently wrote, "Arguments that appeal to something called 'human nature'" are flawed because they "compress such diverse and complex phenomena into such a flat, colorless cartoon that erases most of the things that scholars wish to understand."[6] Human nature, in this view, is a discredited idea heavily laden with excessive historical and political baggage and therefore remains analytically suspect. Cronon goes on to say that the concept of human nature, "assumes as an uncontested fact that humanity can be captured in a single monolithic description."[7] This insightful observation succinctly describes the way most humanists think about this idea. Ironically, this concise dismissal of one antiquated semantic construct comes to the reader in a five-hundred-page book dedicated to deconstructing another equally antiquated semantic construct, "nature."

Tossed onto the slag heap by most social scientists, the idea of "human nature" continues to leech out, like cyanide from an abandoned mine, into the popular discourse influencing understandings of human behavior and perceptions of the environment. Many historians, philosophers, and anthropologists would readily support the argument for putting the idea of human nature to rest. Still, intelligent people continue to find naive versions of the concept of human nature particularly tantalizing. Books, articles, and philosophies that reduce complex human relationships and behaviors to a set of easily understandable biological imperatives consistently top best-seller lists and make headlines in American papers.[8]

Failure to acknowledge and explore the ways these assumptions work in organizing human and environmental politics jeopardizes the project of environmentalism and environmental history. Proponents of the environmental justice movement have understood this for some time, arguing that notions of human nature often dictate environmental politics. With this in mind we set out to construct a book that focuses on theory, history, and human nature. The essays that follow explore the tangled roots of this compelling, provocative, and controversial concept from a variety of perspectives. All those involved in this project shared a belief in the importance of uncovering ideas of human nature that hide between the lines of environmental history and environmental politics.

Despite the silence from environmental scholars on the subject of human nature, this analysis is not without a significant historical precedent. Beginning with the publication of Darwin's *On the Origin of Species* in 1859, social theorists have looked to biological explanations for human social and political development. From Herbert Spencer's mid-nineteenth-century applications of social Darwinism to E. O. Wilson's idea of sociobiology, the belief that natural selection and genetic competition determine the most important characteristics of human behavior has remained a popular and persistent theme.[9] The search for basic human traits and the attempt to define and explain a fundamental "nature" dates to classical antiquity.

Most notably, generations of philosophers explored and debated the idea of human nature for centuries. Separating the human from the nonhuman, these thinkers tried to fashion a framework for understanding the relationship between the natural and the divine. Imagining the world around them as physical, material, and "fixed," governed by scientific principles often called "laws," these philosophers assigned rigid hierarchies to explain the range of all human behavior. The Enlightenment only intensified this investigation. By rejecting the theological basis for viewing nature and human nature, writers like Thomas Hobbes and David Hume tried to find "overarching discourses" through which the "objective reality" of human nature "could be defined and expressed."[10] Driven by a strong faith in objectivity, the search for human constants became a key element in the development of the modern worldview as the discourse of new scientific knowledge seemed to legitimize the existence of a fundamental human nature.[11] Later, the industrial revolution and the rise of the market economy caused social thinkers to once again seek out metanarratives and monolithic categories to analyze and explain an increasingly complicated and chaotic modern world. Social Darwinism and notions of immutable human nature provided seemingly logical explanations for social injustice, racial inequality, and disparities of wealth. Late-nineteenth-century capitalist imperialism and its accompanying notions of "manifest destiny" and "the white man's burden" are just two examples of how ideas of human nature influenced political and economic action. By the beginning of the twentieth century, the progressive ideal of linear evolutionary progress toward a rational and moral telos dominated the discourse on human nature.

As this century progressed, the idea of a universal human nature increasingly came under fire from humanists and social scientists who, more in keeping with Darwin's original intent, began to explore sources of cultural diversity rather than searching for rigid social and cultural hierarchies. For example, sociologists, anthropologists, psychologists, and historians each tried to move beyond the dominant narrative to write particular stories that illustrated how human social life is the product of specific historical and cultural environments, not preordained by a biologically determined hierarchy. The uncritical use of value-laden terms like "nature," "culture," and "human nature" came under further attack from postmodern theorists highly suspicious of tropes that reduced complex historical realities into simplistic models that tended to deny individual agency and contingency. By the mid-1970s scholars from many fields pronounced the idea of human nature officially dead.

The funeral notices were, as it turned out, a little premature, for around the same time a new crop of scholars and philosophers began reviving the corpse. The leader of this resurgence was the distinguished Harvard biologist Edward O. Wilson. In the 1970s Wilson proposed a new philosophy of human nature based on a lifetime of careful research into the social structure of ant communities. In his 1975 book, *Sociobiology: The New Synthesis,* he argued that human behaviors, from love and sharing to hate and anger, have a determined genetic component. While lauded as nothing less than genius by many, Wilson's ideas on gene theory and human nature came under blistering attack by colleagues like Stephen J. Gould, who argued that sociobiology and biological determinism derive from, and help to maintain, particular sociocultural biases and unequal political relationships. Sociobiology, Gould wrote, validates "the potency of biological determinism as a social weapon, for 'others' will be thereby demeaned, and their lower socioeconomic status validated, as a scientific consequence of their innate ineptitude rather than society's unfair choices."[12] Despite the criticism from Gould and others, Wilson's ideas continue to influence the way Americans, including some of the contributors to this volume, think about human behavior and the environmental crisis of the twentieth century.[13]

Although Wilson stands as the leading popular advocate for the genetic study of human behavior, a number of other popular works have recently found an audience. Richard Dawkins's *The Selfish Gene,* published in 1976, rekindled the "nature versus nurture" debate. In a similar fashion, Jared Diamond's *The Third Chimpanzee* (1992) spawned a new wave of public interest in the notion that much of our behavior can be best explained through a systematic study of our genetic kinship with other organisms. While many disagree with Dawkins and Diamond, both of their books represent serious and at times insightful attempts to grapple with complex issues. Less benign was Richard J. Herrnstein and Charles A. Murray's best-selling *The Bell Curve.* Published in 1994, this book proclaimed to have hard evidence for racial inequalities in intelligence. Like Spencer before them, the authors of this widely debated book lapse into the same naturalist fallacy that has dominated much of the popular debate on human nature.[14] For biologist Stephen Jay Gould, the popularity of *The Bell Curve* was proof that the debate about human nature and biological determinism are both "timeless and timely."[15]

While popular works continue to influence social perceptions of difference, the scientific debates in the field of sociobiology have moved far beyond the analytical shortcomings of crude biological determinism. Recent work exploring the evolution of animal societies, for example, illustrates the myriad ways that evolutionary strategies incorporate the influences of environment and historical change. A true understanding of biology, these scholars suggest, does not come from the exploration of fixed genes or essential behaviors but rather through an understanding of species fluidity and change.[16]

Over the years many different disciplines have claimed the idea of human nature as their own. Anthropologists, biologists, and philosophers in particular have spent decades arguing over the worth, or worthlessness, of human nature as a tool. At the same time scholars from a wide variety of disciplines and perspectives have also studied and continue to study this subject. Therefore when we assembled the participants for our human nature conference, we cast our nets wide. The variety of the essays in this collection reflects the interdisciplinary focus of the participants. Because of the complexity of the topic we sought out varied perspectives, drawing on different epistemological traditions and viewpoints. The eclectic, and sometimes argumentative, quality of the essays highlights this emphasis, resulting, we hope, in a whole greater than the sum of its parts. The conclusions of the various authors do not always agree, and that is probably as it should be. Consensus was never the goal. This book represents a beginning, a discussion that raises more questions than it answers. Human nature, like other grand concepts in the western tradition, ultimately defies unanimity. We hope this book will spark further discussion and make a contribution to the ongoing effort to better understand the interrelationship between our cultural perspectives and our biological imperatives.

NOTES

1. Greta Gaard, ed., *Ecofeminism: Women, Animals, Nature* (Philadelphia: Temple University Press, 1993); Carol Bigwood, *Earth Muse: Feminism, Nature, and Art* (Philadelphia: Temple University Press, 1993); and Joni Seager, *Earth Follies: Coming to Feminist Terms with the Global Environmental Crisis* (New York: Routledge, 1993). For an analysis of ideas of human nature in these works, see Virginia Scharff, "Are Earth Girls Easy? Ecofeminism, Women's History, and Environmental History," *Journal of Women's History* 7, no. 2 (summer 1995): 164–75.

2. James Clifford, *The Predicament of Culture: Twentieth-Century Ethnography, Art, and Literature* (Cambridge: Harvard University Press, 1988), 10.

3. This is not to say the idea and its role in influencing popular perceptions and academic scholarship has been ignored by all. Anthropologists and ethnographers have spent the last twenty years engaged in an introspective analysis of how ideas like "culture" and "human nature" influence academic discourse. See, for example, James Clifford and George E. Marcus, eds., *Writing Culture: The Poetics and Politics of Ethnography* (Berkeley: University of California Press, 1986); James Clifford, *The Predicament of Culture*; and Clifford Geertz, *The Interpretation of Cultures* (New York: Basic Books, 1973).

4. William deBuys, *Enchantment and Exploitation: The Life and Hard Times of a New Mexico Mountain Range* (Albuquerque: University of New Mexico Press, 1985); Arthur F. McEvoy, *The Fisherman's Problem: Ecology and the Law in the California Fisheries, 1850–1980* (New York: Cambridge University Press, 1986); Richard White, *The Organic Machine* (New York: Hill & Wang, 1995). There are, of course, many other good examples of environmental historians who make careful analysis of human beings a central part of their ecological histories. See in particular Donald Worster, *Rivers of Empire: Water, Aridity, and the Growth of the American West* (New York: Pantheon, 1985), and William Cronon, *Changes in the Land: Indians, Colonists, and the Ecology of New England* (New York: Hill & Wang, 1983).

5. See, for example, William Cronon, ed., *Uncommon Ground: Toward Reinventing Nature* (New York: Norton, 1995).

6. Ibid., 35.

7. Ibid.

8. Perhaps the most interesting example of the popularity of naive appeals to human

nature can be found in the rhetoric of the 1996 presidential campaign. Members of the Republican party attempted to explain the gender gap by arguing that the Democratic party maintained policies and goals that inherently appealed to innate female characteristics. Ergo, more women supported Clinton than Dole. Despite serious flaws in logic, not the least of which was a failure to look at the history of female voting in past elections, this appeal to fundamental human nature became the Republican party line on the issue of the gender gap, explaining away social, cultural, and individual contingency with a neat biological solution to a pesky problem. Carol Travis, "Misreading the Gender Gap," *New York Times,* September 17, 1996.

9. Spencer lays out his theory of social Darwinism and the "survival of the fittest" in the eighty-volume magnum opus *The System of Synthetic Philosophy, 1862–1893.* An entomologist by training, Edward O. Wilson has produced a long series of essays and books dealing with his ideas of human genetic development and the relation of genetics to society and culture: *Sociobiology: The New Synthesis* (Cambridge: Harvard University Press, 1975); *On Human Nature* (Cambridge: Harvard University Press, 1978); *Biophilia* (Cambridge: Harvard University Press, 1984); with Charles J. Lumsden, *Genes, Mind, and Culture: The Coevolutionary Process* (Cambridge: Harvard University Press, 1981); and with Stephen R. Kellert, *The Biophilia Hypothesis* (Washington, D.C.: Island Press, 1994).

10. Susan M. Pearce, *Museums, Objects, and Collections* (Washington, D.C.: Smithsonian, 1992), 2.

11. Ibid.

12. Stephen Jay Gould, *The Mismeasure of Man,* 2d ed. (New York: Norton, 1996), 27.

13. For example, in the June 17, 1996, issue of *Time* magazine Wilson was included in the magazine's "25 Most Influential People" celebration.

14. Richard Dawkins, *The Selfish Gene* (New York: Oxford University Press, 1976); Jared M. Diamond, *The Third Chimpanzee: The Evolution and Future of the Human Animal* (New York: HarperCollins, 1992); Richard J. Herrnstein and Charles A. Murray, *The Bell Curve: Intelligence and Class Structure in American Life* (New York: Free Press, 1994).

15. *The Mismeasure of Man,* 26.

16. For more on recent trends, see the journal *Evolutionary Biology.*

PART I

Biology and Culture

Although the essays in this volume attack the question of human nature from a wide variety of perspectives, they do share some important similarities and generally fall into two groups. The essays in this first part, by Dan Flores, Virginia Scharff, Vera Norwood, and Max Oelschlaeger, all focus their discussions on issues of evolution, biological determinism, and the cultural construction of nature. Among the questions posed by these authors are the following: How do implicit and explicit ideas of human nature operate in science, and, in turn, how do these ideas filter into environmental discourse? How do gendered assumptions of human nature structure our understandings of nature? To what extent have ideas about biological determinism and sociobiology shaped our understanding of human interaction with the nonhuman world? Finally, what is the relationship between evolution, ecology, and culture? How, in other words, does human history intersect with human biology?

Perhaps the most iconoclastic and thought-provoking essay in this collection is Dan Flores's meditation on sociobiology. Flores argues that environmentalists and other liberals have been drawn to "culture and economics because those are the aspects of human life that . . . can be socially engineered toward perfection." He goes on to say that we should instead pay close attention to concepts of humans as "nature's children." We are, according to Flores, biologically determined to a degree that is uncomfortable for many to accept. Flores asks us to reconsider sociobiology because, as he argues, it can reveal more crucial insights into the current environmental predicament than cultural and economic analysis have provided.

Like Flores, Virginia Scharff takes on conventional wisdom and directly confronts some of the basic assumptions of the field of environmental history. Scharff critiques environmental historians for failing to consider gender seriously in their analysis of human interaction with nature. Behind a mask of inclusion and open-mindedness, Scharff argues, environmental history is dominated by a "residual androcentrism." Moreover, perspectives from women's history and feminist analysis could invigorate and enrich the stories environmental historians tell.

Vera Norwood's illuminating essay examines how the "social construction of gender is implicated in what we find to value and preserve in nature." By stressing the connections between what we value and preserve in nature and how we invent new ways to view the world around us, Norwood examines how the filters of gender, science, and culture affect our view of the nonhuman world. Using naturalists John Burroughs and Florence Merriam Bailey as examples of the divergent ways that men and women approach nature, Norwood illustrates that what we perceive as "natural" is always subject to gendered perceptions and cultural constructions.

Working from a background in environmental ethics, Max Oelschlaeger's essay is among the strongest analyses of the intellectual roots of the idea of human nature. Arguing that as long as history is defined apart from the "biophysical process," then dysfunctional relations between human society and nature will continue and even worsen. The corrective, Oelschlaeger suggests, is simply to accord nature a place within the narrative of history. The result will be a blend of nature and culture where the two are truly interactive, a narrative where nature operates as a genuine agent of change. When history becomes a "narrative of real people rooted in actual places, grappling with the realities of living on and with the land," then human society will finally have a way to know and understand relations with the natural world.

CHAPTER ONE

NATURE'S CHILDREN

Environmental History as
Human Natural History

Dan Flores

How could we *be* were it not for this planet that provided our very shape? Two conditions — gravity and a livable temperature range between freezing and boiling — have given us fluids and flesh. The trees we climb and the ground we walk on have given us give fingers and toes. The "place" . . . gave us far-seeing eyes, the streams and breezes gave us versatile tongues and whorly ears. The land gave us a stride, and the lake a dive. The amazement gave us our kind of mind.
— GARY SNYDER, *The Practice of the Wild*

You will soon find it theologically and factually true that man by nature is a damn mess.
— NORMAN MACLEAN, *A River Runs Through It*[1]

On an invigorating autumn morning in Montana's Bitterroot Valley, with the first big snow of the season draping the sagebrush and the sun angle yet low enough that as frost settles out of the intense blue the heavens seem to be raining glitter, I strap on skis, whistle for my wolf hybrid to join me, and set out across the foothills of the Sapphire Mountains to look for elk. It is one of those incredible daybreaks that in late-twentieth-century human description (or so the thoughts form in my mind) would come across, frankly, as so beautiful, it's almost corny. It's sunrise. It's the Rocky Mountains, with all their associations. We're looking for elk, an animal with a peculiar history in this part of the world that I can conjure with just a little concentration. I'm in Montana, with a meaning different from anywhere else, skiing literally out the door of my house, with big, official wilderness areas in view, accompanied by an animal whose ancestry is three-fourths wolf and who acts it. It's the American West at the turn of the twentieth century, and all those names and thoughts have cultural associations in my head that are coded into the synapses. I couldn't get them out if I wanted to.

We move — I glide, Wily lopes, bounds, and sniffs — our way across foothills covered with Idaho fescue, sagebrush, rabbitbrush, and ponderosa pines, and as I continue my thoughts about this flux we call nature, naming things and experiencing emotions that are equal parts personal and cultural as I do so, I happen to glance at Wily, who appears to be devouring the morning as avidly as I am. We are connected, this part wolf and me, by more than personal history, and skiing along, I begin to tick off the ways. We are both native earthlings, for one, both vertebrate mammals of peculiarly social species, with more in common — more DNA, skeletal, and chemical similarities — than not. We're also both male. We share a hunting past and adaptive plasticity. Our apparatus for apprehending the surrounding world, our sensory organs, are exactly the same even if he relies more on smell and I on sight. The biological drives bequeathed us by natural selection have meant that as species we both have manipulated the world for reasons we barely comprehend.

What does it mean, then, that when I look out at "nature" this bright morning, my cultural associations about it are richer than his? What does it mean to our experiences that I am densely cultured, and he (relative to me) is not? And what meaning can be divined from the fact that I, after all, am only his rather more reflective cousin — that I, too, am an animal?

I believe strongly that for we humans, our animalness may well be the most important thing about us, and that in the twenty-first century recognition of that importance is going to become widely appreciated. But what meaning will we draw from it? For several millennia now, when our animal origins have been acknowledged by history, philosophy, theology, and science, modern western humanity's deeply internalized idea has been that within the animus lies a core of evil. That is implicit (if not frankly acknowledged) in the Judeo-Christian conception of original sin, of humans as "fallen." And in our own time, the notion that pristine nature is a garden of harmony that can only be blighted by our touch is one of the most powerful premises of modern environmentalism.

However ancient the wild nature/human culture dichotomy is — whether it dates to Calvinist disgust with the human body, or to the Judeo-Christian notion that humans alone possess souls, or reaches back even further to the Greek distinction between the earth/body and the heavens/spirit (with its implication of the superiority of the latter), or yet more distantly in our origins to the dawn of individual self-awareness, as Claude Levi-Strauss believed — that we humans are now permanently divorced from nature is a tenet of modern life.[2] That's true no less in the church pews and at the mall than among environmentalists, whose most notable creation in America has been the wilderness system, dedicated to the cultural conceit that the continent was virginal and pure when Europeans arrived and therefore for nature to remain at its best, humans should only be visitors.[3]

A deep and unquestioned Puritanism — humans as evil animals — seems to glare out of these notions, yet they persist. Political scientist Robert Paehlke's prognostication, *Environmentalism and the Future of Progressive Politics,* pulls no punches about the matter: Humans may have evolved on the African savannas and spent ninety-nine percent of our history as hunter-gatherers, but now we should all live in cities and leave nature alone, period. Even historian Roderick Nash, in one of the first issues of *Wild Earth Journal,* proposed a future America that clusters all we humans along the coasts, reserving the interior of the continent as wilderness where our light foraging activities would keep our damage to the natural world to a minimum.[4]

To many of us interested in ideas about nature and humanity, the emergence of environmental history is one of the intriguing seismic stirrings in academics in recent years. But although environmental history takes as its operative premise that at base history ought to be a study of the ecological relationship between humans and the natural world, environmental history actually has not been particularly effective so far in addressing the fundamental fact of humans as animals. Donald Worster's essay "History as Natural History," which calls for an ecological approach to human history similar to the one biologists use with other species, has come closest. But in two more widely read pieces, "Doing Environmental History" and "Seeing Beyond Culture," Worster calls on environmental historians to focus primarily on three levels of analysis: the re-creation of natural ecologies, an examination of human cultural values and ideologies, and an analysis of economics of the type Worster is famous for in books like *Dust Bowl* and *Rivers of Empire.* And in *Dust Bowl* Worster argues that environmental disasters like the collapse of the southern plains in the 1930s cannot be explained by "that vague entity, 'human nature,' but rather by the peculiar culture that shaped their values and actions. It is the hand of culture that selects out innate human qualities and thereby gives variety to history. It was culture in the main that created the Dust Bowl."[5]

The three widely applied approaches Donald Worster has outlined are not the only ways that writers interested in the history of humans and nature have framed that interaction. One of the most useful ways to think about and write environmental histories has always been through a kind of bioregional lens, commencing with a place that seems to hang together ecologically or hydrologically and tracing human adaptations to it over the *longue durée.* In the American West this tradition dates at least to Walter Prescott Webb's *The Great Plains: A Study in Institutions and Environment* (1931) and to James Malin's various works on the Kansas prairies in the 1940s and 1950s. Some might argue that their premises borrowed heavily from Frederick Jackson Turner and in turn from Darwin, since bioregional history is nothing if not

Darwinian: in other words, humans considered as ecosystem animals making adjustments to particular habitats.[6] Some of the best modern books written by environmental historians, considering regional human cultures as a kind of "adaptive package" to places, have followed this approach. I've attempted to keep environmental history at least nominally pointed toward work like this and have argued that the field's intellectual roots in the western history work of Turner, Webb, and Malin are in fact Darwinian, bioregional, and interested in "place" above all.[7]

Probably because of the back-to-back success within humanism of, first, materialist Marxist theory and later cultural relativism — along with the lingering power of the old notion that humans have somehow escaped nature — late-twentieth-century environmental history has mostly continued to follow the path Worster and Nash laid out for it. In other words, what has really pushed historical writing so far are works on how people and places have been integrated into the global capitalist economy, a narrative that has become almost formulaic: Start with pristine nature, add noble primitives who coexist blissfully with the world, introduce the white capitalists, and watch nature and natives go shit-bang in nothing flat. It's Rudyard Kipling history with a conscience.

Or, in the big wake of Nash's *Wilderness and the American Mind* (and more recently William Cronon's controversial edited anthology, *Uncommon Ground*), historians of the environment have done the postmodern dance with culture whereby the natural world as a concrete reality (and presumably our evolution in it) disappears into the shimmer of cultural diversity and all the various words and symbols we humans use to explain the world. It is difficult to locate the human animal, fashioned by evolution and still carrying genetic imperatives within us, in either of these approaches. The only major attempt to revise the Worster/Nash model, by Carolyn Merchant, has merely argued that women and reproduction shouldn't be left out of the analysis. Merchant's *Ecological Revolutions* is an excellent example of how the addition of gender studies, useful and needed as it is, mostly amounts to a gloss on the same old story.[8]

Watching my wolf hybrid investigate the Bitterroot Valley this lovely morning and thinking about the two Rocky Mountain valleys in question here — the one that pours through his sensory apparatus and the one that exists in my head — I am thinking that there may be a more fundamental way at least to *think* about the stories that make up environmental history, in the American West or any other place. It's a way that takes a step beyond even bioregional history and into a realm that precious few of us seem to embrace or much want to hear about. But what about looking at human history by commencing with a frank and open acknowledgment that at core we *are* animals like any other, motivated by impulses that are hundreds of thousands of years old, impulses that our cultural overlays have conspired to conceal but that influence the way we interact with the world in profound ways? Ways we ought to be up front about.

Environmentalists and other liberals, humanist and activist to a fault, have naturally been drawn to culture and economics because those are aspects of human life that seem reformable, that can be socially engineered toward perfection. Indeed, by insisting that the world exists only in the form of words and ideas arising in the human brain, postmodernism implies that *simply by an act of the human imagination* we can create any kind of world we want. Competitive struggle, violence, technological overreach, human stresses on nature all can be reformed and probably eliminated by collective acts of human will. Or so one would assume.

Reading the recent anthology *Ecopsychology: Restoring the Earth, Healing the Mind,* in search of clues among those conversant with Jung and his "collective unconscious" and Freud's *Civilization and Its Discontents*[9] for an underlying animalness that history has failed to reach, I have been struck by the realization that even ecopsychologists place all their hopes for "healing" in tinkering with the institutions enveloping us. Blow up your TV, they say. Raise male children differently, they say. Stop going to the mall and being a pawn to conspicuous consumption, they say. Just say no. And in essay after essay they tell us to look for models of environmentally correct behavior in the preindustrial, precapitalist, "preconsumer," "pretechnological" primary cultures of hunters and gatherers and subsistence agriculturists. New Mexico psychologist Chellis Glendinning, one of the contributors, has published a book with a title that sums up the ecopsychology gestalt: *My Name Is Chellis and I'm in Recovery from Western Civilization.* Every contributor's assumption — perhaps this is endemic to ecopsychology — emerges unquestioning out of the Freudian premise that because civilization has caused us to repress the animal within, modern human nature is "sick."[10]

Perhaps it is. But I wonder. Reading fairly broadly in history and studying Native American environmental history more closely have left me more than mildly skeptical of a tenet of faith among cultural interpreters: that there is a golden age of environmental balance and harmony in the human past and that all we have to do to create environmental sustainability is to pirate those ancient lessons. Everyone conversant with Paul Shepard's arguments knows that since *The Tender Carnivore and the Sacred Game* (1973), he has been arguing that the Neolithic revolution of six thousand to ten thousand years ago was the true "fall" of humanity from ecological grace into ecological madness. As he puts it flatly in a recent essay, "Once, our species did live in stable harmony with the natural environment. . . . "[11] Thus what is really fundamental to regaining environmental sanity is a recultivation of what Max Oelschlaeger calls the "paleolithic consciousness."[12]

Hmmm . . . I peruse Shepard's books, and nowhere can I find an explanation from him for why that ten-thousand-year-old Neolithic revolution of agriculture and domestication occurred in the first place if things were so good and stable before it. Or why the previous fifteen thousand years of human history had featured so rapid a spread of humans out of Africa, Europe, and Asia into Australia, New Zealand, the Americas, and virtually every island chain in the Pacific. Or why the extinctions of so many hundreds of species in the archeological record—the list is an enormous one—dovetail so with the appearance of human hunters in all those places they'd never been before.[13] What Shepard sees as ancient sanity and sustainability and so many of his readers accept so uncritically, I confess I interpret as the record of a species that had reached the limits of population using an ever more sophisticated hunter-gatherer technology. I confess I have to look hard at these stories to find much reassurance that environmental "sanity" merely requires ransacking the past for a cultural or economic magic bullet.[14]

While history has paid little or no attention to the concept of humans as nature's children, philosophy—particularly the philosophy of deep ecology—is one academic discipline that has. Because I think it is essential to accept the human animal legacy, I am intuitively drawn to deep ecology. But I find several of its premises unexamined and unsupported, and probably insupportable. Basic to deep ecology is the existence, laid out by the work of Marshall Sahlins, Shepard, and others, of a hunter-gatherer ecological golden age for humans that we must somehow recapture.[15] But deep ecology philosophers have made no effort to confirm the very foundation of their philosophy. In fact, the study of past cultures, both hunting and agricultural, does present some examples of societies that sustained themselves over long spans of time but within a longer term and broader pattern of steadily mounting human population and environmental overreach, along with some world-class collapses and human-caused biodiversity simplifications.

Nor has deep ecology been systematic about which features of hunter-gatherer cultures we should learn from. If it's population control, then the lessons aren't reassuring ones: Hunter-gatherer population regulation often centered on expedients, like killing up to forty percent of female infants at birth, that seem overly draconian by modern standards. And the trajectory of *longue durée* history indicates that as a whole, humans have never been able to keep a lid on our populations, leading to the human colonization of every nook and cranny of the globe by eleven thousand years ago and finally to the agricultural revolution. By the time the colonization of the planet by hunters-gatherers was complete, human numbers stood at four million. They had risen to five million by the initial stages of the Neolithic revolution and then, as small-scale subsistence agriculture and the settled lifestyle spread across Eurasia, mushroomed to fifty million by 3000 B.P. The organization of states pushed the global population to a hundred million by the time of Christ and to two hundred million by A.D. 200.[16]

Or is a simpler technology the lesson deep ecologists want us to draw from a supposed environmental golden age? If so, its philosophers are silent on the historical evidence for the rapid technological diffusion and adoption of new tools among most primary cultures, one exemplified by the virtually universal scramble to acquire metal implements and tools with the arrival of traders from the industrialized market. Where, one wonders, along the lengthy but connected trail that follows toolmaking out of the prehuman primate's rocks and sticks to our bulldozers and the World Wide Web, should we or could we have stopped? Judged by the human impact on the nonhuman world, the Clovis tool kit that helped push hundreds of megafaunal species to their extinctions in the Americas ten thousand years ago was too much technology. E. O. Wilson believes that since humans evolved, we have reduced the number of bird species around the planet by approximately 25 percent. Most of those losses came not in the twentieth century but in the first waves of human migrations ten thousand years ago.[17]

Animistic religions, apparently so different from Judeo-Christianity by virtue of their premise that humans are not unique, are universally assumed to be the key to supposed primary culture success. But deep ecology misses the mark here, too, by too dogmatically believing that Lynn White Jr.'s 1967 argument about anthropocentrism in Christianity and western science is the one big insight that explains modern environmental crises.[18] Deep ecology adherents have thus insisted that primary religions were biocentric rather than anthropocentric. I think most anthropologists and historians — even those like Adrian Tanner or Richard Nelson, who have supported the idea that primary cultures were ecologically sustainable — believe it would be more accurate to say that animistic religions accord admirable respect to entities outside the human sphere but that like those of New Mexico's pueblo Indians, the ceremonial lives and cosmologies of most primary cultures are actually extremely human centered. The goal is to keep the world working smoothly so that humans and their descendants can continue to inhabit it and live the good life.[19] In fact, much of the work long used to support the idea that animistic religions and population control were at the heart of primary culture environmental sensitivity — among them Harvey Feit's widely used "The Ethno-Ecology of the

Wasanipi Cree; or How Hunters Can Manage Their Resources"[20] — has been critiqued in recent years by anthropologists testing a more materialist model borrowed from biology, called optimal foraging strategy. In a 1982 volume titled *Resource Managers: North American and Australian Hunter-Gatherers,* Annette Hamilton writes:

> The romanticized image of the hunter-gatherer as the original conservationist was propagated in the mid-1970s. The fact that these societies all possessed strong sentiments of connection to the natural world, although expressed in different ways, lent support to the view that they had remained in a stable relationship to their resource base. This was achieved not merely because there were few of them but because they took care to regulate their utilization of the products of the land, informed always by their respect for nature. There is much truth in this stereotype. The precise mechanisms, however, by which such regulation could occur is a much more difficult question to answer. . . . It is easy to assert that something approaching conservation was going on, but much harder to demonstrate it convincingly.[21]

In fact, optimal foraging strategy asserts that what appears to be "conservation" among hunting peoples was actually a by-product of attempting to maximize hunting efficiency and use of time. Thus hunter-gatherers ignored depleted habitats and placed taboos on certain species not to achieve conservation but in search of maximum yield for minimum effort. As wildlife populations shrink, this hypothesis argues, hunters actually hunt more, and they range farther afield. These are assertions that historical evidence buttresses. Anthropologist Raymond Hames has proposed that *the* test for conservation as an adaptation is whether, if conservation is the result of some practice, it is occurring *by design*. His careful study of hunting among the modern Yanomamo "casts doubt on the existence of conservation in lowland Amazonia." Similarly anthropologist Robert Brightman has concluded that the precontact Cree "respected" animals but lacked a general concept of animal population dynamics. As for religion, he makes the startling claim that because it taught the Cree that animals regenerated — the Cree idea was *akwanaham otoskana,* or "animal covers its bones" — and fostered the belief that it was arrogance to assume that animal numbers could be influenced through human manipulation, among the Cree, religion would have encouraged unregulated hunting rather than acting as a brake.[22]

While I believe that for the sake of ideology, deep ecologists are denying primary peoples' history and humanity and toying with the romantic attractions of the past, deep ecology is probably on its soundest footing when it promotes the primary culture tie to local ecosystems through bioregional living. But again, this philosophy's foundation of anti-agriculturalism is a problem. It seems not to have occurred to deep ecology philosophers, aware of and perplexed by ecofeminism's suspicions of them, that their attack on the Neolithic revolution as humanity's fall from ecological grace is an attack on the feminization of culture.[23] Agriculture has its origins in the plants that women gathered. And women—as I can attest from observing the difference in the way Wily reacts to human gender—are believed to have been critical players in the domestication of animals as well.

My suspicion from this exercise is that environmental history (not to mention ecopsychology and philosophy) is going to have to investigate humanness at a deeper level even than culture or materialist economics to understand some of the reasons our species interacts with the world around us the way we do. Horrifying as it is to think, just as my wolf hybrid has a wolf nature that no amount of socialization can erase, we humans appear to have a human nature beneath all that rich cultural overlay. So I have come to think that an incorporation of what once was called sociobiology, and now thrives in a field called evolutionary psychology, into history—a consideration of we humans as "the third chimpanzee," to borrow Jared Diamond's phrase—may help us to a better understanding of ourselves and the arc of our environmental past.

What good will it do us to acknowledge forces within that may be harder to alter than a bad law or flawed institution? It seems to me that understanding the animal within may be fundamental to socialization in whatever form. And more, it tends to portray us not as having possessed a "sane" childhood as a species, now "alienated" or gone mad, but in a continuum, as a species doing now exactly what evolution so precisely selected us to do all along. The causes of twentieth-century environmental decay aren't human insanity or our tools or our economics; those are only the cultural symptoms. The causes of the human assault on the world—and, conversely and ironically, the sources of our hope for ourselves and a biologically diverse planet, too—are evolutionary and mammalian. The foundation of all of it seems to lie in our hardwiring.

The modern fields of study that have attempted to explain human behavior within an evolutionary framework, sociobiology and evolutionary psychology, are usually said to have had their origins with E. O. Wilson's two seminal works, *Sociobiology: The New Synthesis* in 1976 and *On Human Nature* in 1978, and Richard Dawkins's *The Selfish Gene*, which also saw print in 1976.[24] In fact, the foundation of the study of humans as animals actually dates to Darwin's *The Expression of Emotions in Man and Animals* (1872) and *The Descent of Man and Selection in Relation to Sex* (1874).[25] But it was

Wilson who most clearly recognized the challenge sociobiology threw up to contemporary cultural determinism. He wrote in *On Human Nature* that "we are biological," but that accepting this is horribly deflating for a species that had so long thought of itself as unique, outside nature, and possessed of free will. If "our souls cannot fly free," Wilson wrote in 1978, then we have no place to go but earth.[26]

In the century between the appearance of Darwin's works and Wilson's, outrage at public discussion of the idea that humans were animals had if anything grown more shrill. Interestingly, in both the 1870s and the 1970s it was not so much religious conservatives as liberals who reacted most vigorously. Outrage in the nineteenth century over Herbert Spencer's social Darwinism, purporting to explain the emergence of America's "captains of industry" as the operation of natural selection in human affairs, was a classically liberal position. And so too it was liberals, Marxists, and feminists who reacted to Wilson's books with venomous hostility and charges of biological determinism. For a few years two decades ago sociobiological researchers found themselves in the unique position of being rejected by conservatives who resisted evolution and by liberals who emphasized free will and the cultural perfectibility of humanity. Their papers were unwelcome in many academic journals, and some realized, as one sociobiologist put it, "that we were involved in an enterprise worse than studying the occult; we were [assumed to be] fellow-traveling with the American Nazi party."[27] The reaction to sociobiology was paralleled at the same time and for some of the same reasons by a rejection of the post–World War II anthropological position on human origins known as the "killer ape" or hunting hypothesis and its replacement with the idea of the ecological hunter-gatherer.[28]

Wilson's position over the years has been refined but not reformed. His views in *On Human Nature* were that social scientists were engaging in rampant anthropocentrism by insisting that culture took humans outside nature, and he has not changed his mind. Genetic evolution of human social behavior, he argued, is the product of five million years, culture mostly the product of the past ten thousand. Thus his metaphor, borrowed from Conrad Waddington, of human behavior as a ball tumbling through a landscape from highlands to a shore, with steep, sharply trenched biological topography high up, flattening to meandering, coiling topography low down where culture predominates.

That metaphor led Wilson to disagree with culturalists that human behavior is infinitely plastic, and he pointed out that much of our social behavior (band-type social groupings of ten to a hundred, sexual dimorphism, self-awareness, tool use, cultures that pass along information) is shared with other primates.

Wilson also pointed out that all human cultures share biologically derived patterns that relate directly to ecology, including ethnobotany, food taboos, population policies, property rights, soul concepts, and a desire to control weather. Evolutionary behavior, he asserted, should be the most general and least rational in our repertoire — things like incest taboos, infanticide, aggression, territoriality, and sexual practices. The human instinct for aggression, for example, resides much in territoriality and protection of our ecology, with conflict aimed at "them."

In 1978 Wilson believed that what sociobiology would enable social scientists to achieve was what physics had achieved: a discipline (human history) that was "predictive."[29] By 1993, in an essay called "Is Humanity Suicidal?," Wilson was ready to venture predictions:

> Darwin's dice have rolled badly for Earth. It was a misfortune for the living world, in particular, many scientists believe, that a carnivorous primate and not some more benign form of animal made the breakthrough [to intelligence]. Our species retains hereditary traits that add greatly to our destructive impact. We are tribal and aggressively territorial . . . and oriented by selfish sexual and reproductive drives. Cooperation beyond the family and tribal levels comes hard. Worse, our liking for meat causes us to use the sun's energy at low efficiency. . . . The human species is, in a word, an environmental hazard. . . . Perhaps a law of evolution is that intelligence usually extinguishes itself.[30]

Wilson's conclusion was that we are not suicidal but that survival — especially in a world where biodiversity is preserved — will entail "a reconsideration of our self-image as a species."[31] In recent work he has also further refined the idea (first introduced in *On Human Nature*) that culture itself is biological and that much of our behavior exists as a "bio-cultural" loop where certain cultural traits are selected by the genes for their survivability — religions that proffer ecological advantage, for example.[32]

In its more contemporary form — now known as evolutionary psychology — biological interpretations of human behavior skirt some of the ecological questions Wilson raised in favor of a more narrow focus on what's called the "maximization principle." The argument, presented in the form of the so-called modern synthesis (which some researchers have touted as literally a new Copernican revolution) is that "the universe of biological organization is a system of genetic matter in motion obeying the immanent, natural laws of natural selection and genetic variation."[33] In other words, the most deeply internalized prime directive of all biological species is genetic reproduction and survival, and a great deal of what we gendered species do is propelled (without our realization) by sexuality operating on our selfish genes.

"An important principle in EP," two recent researchers write, referring to evolutionary psychology, "is that there is a human nature: the human brain is composed of a large number of psychological adaptations that are virtually identical across people everywhere."[34] Among the "immanent, natural laws" to which the genes bend us are ecological ones (like territoriality), but it is the sexual ones of our gendered species that have come in for closest study. This deep hardwiring includes a "male strategy" for procuring mates, through which human evolution has favored males who are successful in marshaling and controlling natural resources; a "female strategy" that maximizes reproductive potential among females with the selection of high-status mates and at least some encouragement of partnership stability for child rearing; and a genetic bias in favor of close kin.[35]

One of the aspects of evolutionary psychology that continues to intrigue everyone is exactly what the evolutionary adaptive environment (it even bears its own acronym, EAE) that provides us with all these ancient cues might have been. Wilson early asserted this would be found among forest-dwelling primates, and some researchers still look for ancestral clues to our behavior there. But others think our most telling EAEs were the Pleistocene savannas of our long hunting-gathering past as *Homo sapiens*.[36]

One of the most intriguing joinings of ideas about the human evolutionary adaptive environment with modern environmentalism comes from Wilson's 1984 book, titled *Biophilia: The Human Bond with Other Species*.[37] More recently he and Stephen Kellert have edited *The Biophilia Hypothesis* (1993), an eclectic anthology of papers examining the viability of Wilson's premise that our evolution has bequeathed us an "innate tendency to focus on life and lifelike processes."[38]

The preliminary studies in biophilia and biophobia research seem to show in rather striking ways that it is ludicrous to think that humans ever stepped outside nature. Biophilia and biophobia remind us how rooted our social behavior is in the primate world. Studies of inherited biophobic responses (to snakes and spiders, for example) as well as what appear to be genetic preferences in humans for savannas, parklands, certain tree shapes, and terrain scales that mimic our evolutionary home in east Africa center both our fear of the natural world and also our settlement strategies (and even our aesthetics) in adaptations selected by evolution over deep time. There are also some clear gender differences. Studies using landscape art and architectural landscaping, for example, indicate that men worldwide respond most positively to depictions of open, parklike terrain with distant views, women to scenes of closed canopies and protected settings. One of the contributors to *The Biophilia Hypothesis*, Robert Ulrich, concludes that genetic biophilias and biophobias may be 20 to 40 percent determinative but that most appear to require triggering by learning.[39]

These days two of the most accessible recent books synthesizing the biological position on human history are Jared Diamond's *The Third Chimpanzee* (1992) and Robert Wright's *The Moral Animal* (1994).[40] Historians particularly ought to appreciate biologist Diamond's *longue durée* approach to human history as natural history. As for Wright's journalistic but sound synthesis of evolutionary psychology, its major contribution is an explanation of one of the most troublesome of sociobiology's problems: If the entire biological world is blueprinted around replication of the selfish gene, how can altruism and human morality be explained? The answer, worked out by two of the founders of sociobiology, Robert Trivers and Robert Axelrod, is reciprocity, expressed by game theory's demonstration of how cooperation could evolve in nature, with rewards that enhance individual success through cooperation and an ethical code to govern it. Canadian game theorist Anatol Rapoport's famous "Tit for Tat" (or, do unto others . . .) is thought to most closely represent how reciprocity, altruism, and morality evolved in a selfish gene world.[41] Freud, Wright argues, accurately saw that human inner conflicts result from the animal brain trying to cope with social life, but Freud erred in thinking that the conflict was between the animal and *civilization,* that "primitive man was better off in knowing no restrictions of instinct." In fact, Wright says, it has been a very, very long time since humans knew no restrictions on instincts. The conflict is between instinct and human *societies* of every kind.[42]

Alongside these works, of course, has long existed the view that the richness of human history — at least shallow time history of the sort most all of us are accustomed to reading — would be reduced to a cartoon if interpreted through the lens of biology. Can we profitably reduce the strivings of Horace Tabor in helping fashion the mining economy of nineteenth-century Colorado to a masculine compulsion to marshall resources so as to attract the notice of Baby Doe, a genetically superior mate? Should we dismiss Lewis and Clark's educational and cultural preparations and explain their fascination with the high plains and Rocky Mountain foothills by noting their similarity to the evolutionary adaptive environment of east Africa? Is Mormon polygamy best explained as the male sexual strategy triumphant (or an adaptation of the female strategy to a shortage of males) or by studying Mormon theology or the Mormon communal economy? The cultural anthropologist Marvin Harris once critiqued the "reductionist principles of sociobiology" as underestimating "by several orders of magnitude" the novelty of culture, since it substituted rapid learning for the slow operation of genetic feedback loops. More, while territoriality and gendered sexuality might exist, culture (as history so richly demonstrates) is capable of socializing us into almost any kind of behavior.[43] Further, shouldn't we be a bit suspicious of a science that seems to confirm and buttress the gender status quo?

I suspect that it is in thinking about *longue durée* human history and environmental history, and rarely shallow time histories of specific events, that the new notions of humans as merely another species will be most worthwhile. Perhaps the specific place marker where a consideration of human-history-as-natural-history can help immediately is in addressing what our own culture actually tells us to *think* about human nature.

Early in *Steppenwolf,* German writer Herman Hesse's surrealistic novel of the 1920s, Hesse characterizes his protagonist this way: He calls himself part wolf, part man. . . . With the man he packs in everything spiritual and sublimated or even cultivated to be found in himself and with the wolf all that is instinctive, savage, and chaotic.[44]

Viewed across the great expanse of *longue durée* history, Steppenwolf's dilemma is the most uniquely human of all of evolution's dilemmas. According to Genesis, in the beginning, nature was benign. Then sin came into the world, and with it evil, and the Fall. To Darwinists, however, the classic sins of gluttony, lust, greed, envy, and anger are all stripped-down expressions of impulses emerging out of evolutionary natural selection and the operation of the selfish gene. This dark view of human nature puts modern environmentalists, in particular, in a real box of a dilemma, since it seems to be a non sequitur to think of humans as destroyers and parasites on the earth (the sources of those destructive tendencies lying in human evolutionary history) while "nature" itself is seen as divine and harmonious. And of course such a view makes it all the more difficult to imagine past societies, where presumably human nature was even rawer and more exposed than under the present constraints imposed by religion and the state, as existing in a golden age of ecological harmony.[45]

History seen this way sets up the primary function of socialization all along as the sublimation of the animal appetites, the seven deadly sins, to cultivate a reciprocal altruism that mediates both power relations and the use of nature.[46] Religions and environmental regulations limit the selfish gene's freedom of action, which is why every anarchist militiaman in the West has a bizarre conception of religion and the purest of hatreds for the state.

The conclusion that could be drawn for environmental history is that at the turn of the twenty-first century, we are engaging the world around us with exactly the same selfish genes, exactly the same sexually based prime directive, precisely the mental and sensory apparatus that evolution bequeathed *Zinjanthropus, Homo erectus, Homo habilis,* and every one of our more recent hunting and gathering (and ranching, farming, and investment banking) ancestors — and that we are oblivious to our motives because natural selection designed us to be.[47] Seen in this light, modern environmental history is manifestly not a history of a godlike creature gone over the edge of sanity, but the story of a wildly successful species that has been doing the same things, and for the same reasons, for three million years. It's the history of a species that late in its evolution has assumed that it has stepped outside the external limits nature usually imposes on efflorescence and now doesn't recognize the ancient imperatives, doesn't believe it should be chary of them, or can't muster a resolve to resist their darker implications.

Max Oelschlaeger has argued that humans are biologically underdetermined, culturally overdetermined.[48] While I concur that this view is applicable to what we usually view as the proper subjects of human history, it seems to me that environmental history presents a more naked expression of human biology in action than any other kind of history. If I am right that the reason we have not been able to stop the destruction of nature in our time is because we refuse to recognize the animal within, then externally delivered checks are what we can expect. Checks like new disease epidemics running rampant through overcrowded populations. Massive die-offs from starvation caused by ecological overreach. Wars over resources. And perhaps ultimately an imposed, top-down environmental fascism to keep us from destroying ourselves. All these kinds of fates except the last afflict other animals. We have stories like this in modern human affairs. We call them science fiction.

On the other hand, if Wilson and others are correct and a real biophilia does lie there in our animal origins, it may be that biocultural evolution has only now proceeded to the point of allowing it full expression, that the golden age is in our future rather than in our past. There can be no doubt at all that embracing our animalness, recognizing and confronting the role our long evolution plays in modern human behavior, is a critical step. Once we take it, and perhaps see human nature (like nature itself) not as a mess but as the true and positive core of what it means to be human, then our innate biophilia may be fully triggered. If our cultures *are* able to call up the best from the animal within so that we can puzzle a way through our dilemmas, then our instincts for territory, for living and interacting in local places where feedback loops are short and the world looms about us in sacred detail, will surely be key.

The crux of biological human nature as cause in history is that, read negatively, it gives us no hope. But there is a positive reading that gives us, the mountains and plains west, and the world a chance for a future with dignity. We do, after all, have history, and history gives us the opportunity to let our genes in on the recognized dangers — and the wondrous potential — of being animal.

NOTES

1. Gary Snyder, "The Place, the Region, and the Commons," in *Gary Snyder, The Practice of the Wild: Essays by Gary Snyder* (San Francisco: North Point Press, 1990), 29; Norman Maclean, *A River Runs Through It and Other Stories* (Chicago: University of Chicago Press, 1976).

2. See Alice Ingerson, "Tracking and Testing the Nature-Culture Dichotomy," in *Historical Ecology: Cultural Knowledge and Changing Landscapes,* ed. Carole Crumley (Santa Fe: School of American Research Press, 1994), 43–66.

3. See especially William Cronon, ed., *Uncommon Ground: Toward Reinventing Nature* (New York: Norton, 1995); William Cronon, "The Trouble with Wilderness," *New York Times Magazine* 13 August 1995, 42–45.

4. Robert Paehlke, *Environmentalism and the Future of Progressive Politics* (New Haven: Yale University Press, 1989), 249–51. Roderick Nash first developed his anti-bioregionalist stance in his *Wilderness and the American Mind,* 3d ed. (New Haven: Yale University Press, 1982), 380–84. Donald Worster argues for a foundation for American environmentalism in Puritanism in "John Muir and the Roots of American Environmentalism," in *The Wealth of Nature: Environmental History and the Ecological Imagination* (New York: Oxford University Press, 1993), 184–202.

5. Worster, *The Wealth of Nature,* 30–44; Worster, "Doing Environmental History," in *The Ends of the Earth: Perspectives on Modern Environmental History* (New York: Cambridge University Press, 1988), 289–307; Worster, "Seeing Beyond Culture," *Journal of American History* 76 (March 1990): 1132–36.

6. Walter Prescott Webb, *The Great Plains: A Study in Institutions and the Environment* (Boston: Ginn and Co., 1931); James Malin, *History and Ecology,* ed. Robert Swierenga (Lincoln: University of Nebraska Press, 1985).

7. Dan Flores, "Place: An Argument for Bioregional History," *Environmental History Review* 18 (winter 1994): 1–18. On human adaptation and humans as part of ecosystems, see Roy Rappaport, "Maladaptation in Social Systems," in *The Evolution of Social Systems,* ed. J. Friedman and M. J. Rowlands (London: Duckworth, 1977): 69–71; and in the same volume Anne Whyte, "Systems as Perceived: A Discussion of 'Maladaptation in Social Systems,'" 73–78, and Rappaport, "Normative Modes of Adaptive Processes: A Response to Anne Whyte," 79–88. Also Donald Hardesty, "Rethinking Cultural Adaptation," *The Professional Geographer* 38 (February 1986): 11–18; and Mark McDonnell and Stewart Pickett, eds., *Humans as Components of Ecosystems* (New York: Springer-Verlag, 1993).

8. Carolyn Merchant, *Ecological Revolutions: Nature, Gender, and Science in New England* (Chapel Hill: University of North Carolina Press, 1989), and "Gender and Environmental History," *Journal of American History* 76 (March 1990): 1117–21.

9. Sigmund Freud, *Civilization and Its Discontents*, trans. James Strachey, (New York: Norton, 1961).

10. Theodore Roszak, Mary Gomes, and Allen Kanner, eds., *Ecopsychology: Restoring the Earth, Healing the Mind* (San Francisco: Sierra Club Books, 1995).

11. Ibid., Paul Shepard, "Nature and Madness," 23. Shepard's original expression of these ideas was in *The Tender Carnivore and the Sacred Game* (New York: Scribners, 1973). For a more recent treatment of his on the topic, see "A Post-Historic Primitivism," in *The Wilderness Condition: Essays on Environment and Civilization*, ed. Max Oelschlaeger (Washington: Island Press, 1992), 40–89.

12. Max Oelschlaeger, *The Idea of Wilderness: From Paleolithic Times to the Present* (New Haven: Yale University Press, 1991), 1–30.

13. The literature here is vast, but see particularly Clive Ponting, *A Green History of the World: The Environment and the Collapse of Great Civilizations* (New York: St. Martin, 1991), 18–67; Paul Martin and Henry Wright, eds., *Pleistocene Extinctions: The Search for a Cause* (New Haven: Yale University Press, 1967); Paul Martin and Richard Klein, eds., *Quaternary Extinctions: A Prehistoric Revolution* (Tucson: University of Arizona Press, 1984); and Jared Diamond, "Man the Exterminator," *Nature* 298 (1982): 787–89.

14. See Dan Flores, "Bison Ecology and Bison Diplomacy: The Southern Plains from 1800 to 1850," *Journal of American History* (September 1991): 465–85.

15. See especially George Sessions, preface and introduction to "What Is Deep Ecology?" in *Deep Ecology for the 21st Century: Readings on the Philosophy and Practice of the New Environmentalism*, ed. George Sessions (Boston: Shambhala Press, 1995): ix–xxviii, 3–7. Also Richard Lee and Irven Devore, eds., *Man the Hunter* (New York: Aldine de Gruyter, 1968); Marvin Harris and Eric Ross, eds., *Food and Evolution* (Philadelphia: Temple University Press, 1987); and David McDonald, "Food Taboos: A Primitive Environmental Protection Agency (South America)," *Anthropos* 72 (1977): 734–48.

16. Ponting in *A Green History of the World*, 20, asserts that hunting and gathering was "without doubt the most successful and flexible way of life adopted by humans and the one that caused the least damage to natural ecosystems." Figures on female infanticide and global populations are also from this work, pp. 18–67.

17. E. O. Wilson, "Biophilia and the Conservation Ethic," in *The Biophilia Hypothesis*, ed. Stephen Kellert and E. O. Wilson (Washington: Island Press, 1993), 21–41.

18. See Lynn White, Jr., "The Historical Roots of Our Ecologic Crisis," in *Ecology and Religion in History*, ed. David and Eileen Spring (New York: Harper & Row, 1974), 15–31; and George Sessions, introduction to "Historical Roots of Deep Ecology," in *Deep Ecology for the 21st Century*, 97–103.

19. Richard Nelson, *Make Prayers to the Raven* (Chicago: University of Chicago Press, 1983) and Adrian Tanner, *Bringing Home Animals: Religious Ideology and Mode of Production of the Mistassini Cree Hunters* (London: C. Hurst, 1979). On the pueblos see Yi-Fu Tuan's *Topophilia: A Study of Environmental Perception, Attitudes, and Values* (Englewood Cliffs: Prentice Hall, 1974), 79–83, and his *Space and Place: The Perspective of Experience* (Minneapolis: University of Minnesota Press, 1977), 91–93. Also Charles Adams, *Origin and Development of the Pueblo Katsina Cult* (Tucson: University of Arizona Press, 1991); Elsie Parsons Clews,

Pueblo Indian Religion, 2 vols. (Chicago: University of Chicago Press, 1939). In *Now That the Buffalo's Gone: A Study of Today's American Indians* (Norman: University of Oklahoma Press, 1983): 97, Alvin Josephy puts it this way: "The lessons of history permeated and guided every aspect of Pueblo lives. Their principal teaching was the necessity of maintaining a harmonious relationship with everything in the world in which they lived. . . . The people's welfare demanded harmony between themselves and the entire spirit world. . . . Only man could upset the balance by doing something wrong. To avoid this, Pueblo society was tightly knit and rigidly conformist, ever watchful against any activity that might violate the Creator's directions. . . . The slightest failure to conduct oneself correctly could upset the balance with nature and harm the whole community."

20. Harvey Feit, "The Ethno-Ecology of the Wasanipi Cree; or, How Hunters Can Manage Their Resources," in *Cultural Ecology,* comp. Bruce Cox (Toronto: University of Toronto Press, 1978), 115–25.

21. Annette Hamilton, "Reflections on Economic Forms and Resource Management," in *Resource Managers: North American and Australian Hunter-Gatherers,* ed. Nancy Williams and Eugene Hunn (Boulder: Westview Press, 1982), 240. See also Raymond Hames, "Game Conservation or Efficient Hunting," in *The Question of the Commons: The Culture and Ecology of Communal Resources,* ed. Bonnie McKay and James Acheson (Tucson: University of Arizona Press, 1987), 92–120.

22. Robert Brightman, "Conservation and Resource Depletion: The Case of the Boreal Forest Algonquians," in *The Question of the Commons,* McKay and Hutcheson, 121–41. See also the seminal review article on optimal foraging strategy by Eric Alden Smith, "Anthropological Applications of Optimal Foraging Theory: A Critical Review," *Current Anthropology* 24 (December 1983): 628–632.

23. See George Sessions, introduction to "Deep Ecology and Ecofeminism, Social Ecology, the Greens, and the New Age," in *Deep Ecology for the 21st Century,* 265–68; Warwick Fox, "The Deep Ecology-Ecofeminism Debate and Its Parallels," ibid., 269–89; Michael Zimmerman, "Feminism, Deep Ecology, and Environmental Ethics," *Environmental Ethics* 9 (1987): 21–44.

24. E. O. Wilson, *Sociobiology: The New Synthesis* (Cambridge: Harvard University Press, 1975), and *On Human Nature* (Cambridge: Harvard University Press, 1978); Richard Dawkins, *The Selfish Gene* (New York: Oxford University Press, 1976).

25. Charles Darwin, *The Expression of Emotions in Man and Animals* (London: Watts and Co., 1872); *The Descent of Man and Selection in Relation to Sex* (New York: A. L. Burt, 1874).

26. Wilson, *On Human Nature,* 1–13.

27. Douglas Kendrik, "Bridging Social Psychology and Sociobiology: The Case of Sexual Attraction," in *Sociobiology and the Social Sciences,* ed. Robert Bell and Nancy Bell (Lubbock: Texas Tech University Press, 1989), 6.

28. Matt Cartmill, *A View to Death in the Morning: Hunting and Nature Through History* (Cambridge: Harvard University Press, 1993), chap. 1. See also Richard Leakey and Roger Lewin, *Origins Reconsidered: In Search of What Makes Us Human* (New York: Doubleday, 1992). The hunting hypothesis is regarded as the first truly Darwinian explanation of the origins of humanity.

29. Wilson, *On Human Nature*, 60–61.

30. Ibid., 20–26 and 208.

31. E. O. Wilson, "Is Humanity Suicidal?" in *In Search of Nature* (Washington: Island Press, 1996), 183–99, quote on pp. 184–86.

32. E. O. Wilson, "Culture as a Biological Product," ibid., 107–26. The essay begins: "This is the essence of the matter as I understand it: culture is ultimately a biological product."

33. Joseph Lopreato, "The Maximization Principle: A Cause in Search of Conditions," in Bell and Bell, *Sociobiology and the Social Sciences*, 119.

34. Randy Thornhill and Steve Gangestad, "The Evolution of Human Sexuality," *Trends in Ecology & Evolution* 11 (February 1996): 98–102, and Deborah Blum, *Sex on the Brain: The Biological Differences Between Men and Women* (New York: Viking Penguin, 1997).

35. Dawkins, *The Selfish Gene*; Kenrick, "Sexual Attraction," in Bell and Bell, *Sociobiology and the Social Sciences*, 5–23; Margo Wilson, "Marital Conflict and Homicide in Evolutionary Perspective," ibid., 45–62; Randy Thornhill and Nancy Wilmsen Thornhill, "The Evolution of Psychological Pain," ibid., 73–103; Susan Essock and Michael McGuire, "Social and Reproductive Histories of Depressed and Anxious Women," ibid., 105–118; Randy Thornhill and Steve Gangestad in "The Evolution of Human Sexuality" (see note 33 above) argue that a "vast body of empirical evidence" supports ideas about women's strategy and men's and that new work in *fantasies* (which shows evolved preferences outside the restrictions placed on actual behavior) also supports those ideas.

36. See Meredith Small, *Female Choices: Sexual Behavior of Female Primates* (Ithaca: Cornell University Press, 1993), and Ruth Mace, "Why Do We Do What We Do?" *Trends in Ecology & Evolution* 10 (January 1995): 4–5.

37. E. O. Wilson, *Biophilia: The Human Bond with Other Species* (Cambridge: Harvard University Press, 1984).

38. Wilson, "Biophilia and the Conservation Ethic," in *The Biophilia Hypothesis*, Kellert and Wilson, 31–41.

39. For my points in the text, see especially Stephen Kellert, "The Biological Basis for Human Values of Nature," 42–69, and Robert Ulrich, "Biophilia, Biophobia, and Natural Landscapes," 73–137. Judith Heerwagen and Gordon Orians, in "Humans, Habitats, and Aesthetics," 150–53, argue that because they are done to elicit emotional responses, landscape paintings are effective formats to test preferences. Women tend to "show a greater affinity for enclosure and protected places than do males." Sexual division of labor had much to do with selection for these preferences in early human history, with males preferring openness because of game and females preferring more vegetated areas likely to yield vegetables and refuge. In a study of paintings by men and women, 52 percent of female paintings had high "refuge symbolism" compared to only 25 percent of male paintings. No horizon was visible in 75 percent of the women's paintings. All in *The Biophilia Hypothesis*, ed. Stephen Kellert and Edward Wilson (Washington: Island Press, 1993).

40. Jared Diamond, *The Third Chimpanzee: The Evolution and Future of the Human Animal* (New York: HarperCollins, 1992), and Robert Wright, *The Moral Animal: The New Science of Evolutionary Psychology* (New York: Pantheon, 1994). Dia-

mond is particularly good in his treatment of "The Golden Age That Never Was," 317–48; also Frans de Waal, *Good Natured: The Origins of Right and Wrong in Humans and Other Animals* (Cambridge: Harvard University Press, 1995).

41. Every first move a player in Tit for Tat makes is for cooperation, and after that it makes exactly the move its opponent made the previous encounter, thus avoiding the costs of too much cooperation and getting exploited. In computer simulations, this strategy defeats every other one.

42. Wright, *The Moral Animal,* 321–25.

43. Marvin Harris, *Cultural Materialism: The Struggle for a Science of Culture* (New York: Random, 1979), 119–140.

44. Herman Hesse, *Steppenwolf* (New York: Holt, Rinehart & Winston, 1963, reprint), 3.

45. Robert Wright, "Science and Original Sin," *Time,* October 28, 1996, 76–77.

46. See Karl Butzer, "Environment, Culture, and Human Evolution," *American Scientist* 65 (1977): 572–84.

47. See Paul Ehrlich and Robert Ornstein, *New World, New Mind* (New York: Doubleday, 1989).

48. Conversation with Max Oelschlaeger, Albuquerque, April 6, 1996.

CHAPTER TWO

MAN AND NATURE!

Sex Secrets of Environmental History

Virginia Scharff

My image of History would have at least two bodies in it, at least two persons talking, arguing, always listening to the other as they gestured at their books; it would be a film, not a still picture, so that you could see that sometimes they wept, sometimes they were astonished, sometimes they were knowing, and sometimes they laughed with delight.
— NATALIE ZEMON DAVIS[1]

I tease and entice you, reader, with this title, "Man and Nature! Sex Secrets of Environmental History." But it is likely I shall disappoint you. If you have read *Masters and Johnson* or the *Kinsey Report,* you know that works that put *sex* in the title seduce the reader with the promise of titillation but deliver the goods in a manner more consistent with school-marms than strippers. So it is with me. In the past, I have worked to create what I have called a "tender coupling" between environmental history, women's history, and feminist analysis, a triple conjunction that the environmental historian Dan Flores memorably called a "ménage à trois."[2] In this essay, however, I come not to supplicate, but to lecture.

My subject is environmental history, which I identify as a body of writing and a set of professional techniques, institutions, and practices, or to use the earthier term of the most distinguished and provocative environmental historian, Donald Worster, environmental history is a "field." According to Worster, this scholarly field "deals with all the interactions people have had with nature in past times."[3] I applaud such an enterprise, but like many fields that exist mostly in the domains of words, thoughts, and paper, the objects buried in *this* field are ideas. I will argue here that environmental history, at present, does not begin to answer Worster's description because buried within it is a sex secret. It remains at present not a story of people and other things but is instead a story of man and nature.

Environmental historians have devoted unending energy to answering the question, "What do we mean by nature?"[4] They have spent a whole lot less time trying to define who or what they mean when they write about *humanity*. The relation between the terms *human* and *nature* in environmental history have, however, endless and intimate connections, as when, in seeking moral and political lessons for humans from the collection of diverse things we call nature, we write about nature as if it were singular, a term parallel and comparable to the singular term *man*.

Critics of the very sciences environmental historians incorporate in their scholarship have demonstrated that categories like "man" and "nature" are not only socially constructed but intellectually and politically salient; the words we use to capture knowledge of our world matter, in the here and now.[5] We should heed critiques of science for practical reasons. Environmental historians often use biology, for example, but biology requires interrogation rather than appropriation. Scholars including Carolyn Merchant, Stephen Jay Gould, Evelyn Fox Keller, Donna Haraway, and Londa Schiebinger have shown how the sociopolitical categories of gender, race, and class construct scientific understandings of who, and what, counts as human, as well as what counts as natural.[6]

I believe that humans are best understood as historical animals. Part of what makes us what we are today is a centuries-long struggle within our species, *Homo sapiens*, over the right to be classed as "human" and therefore to claim legitimate right to the powers and privileges of humanity. Among those powers are the right to speak publicly, the right to possess one's own home, the right to own one's own body.

But pause for a moment over this word *species*, the linguistic emblem of a scientific, biologically based view of humanity. If humans are understood biologically, as a species, it is a tautology to say that knowing humanity means understanding the differences and commonalities between males and females. One common definition of species is "a group of intimately related and physically similar organisms that actually or potentially interbreed and are less commonly capable of fertile interbreeding with members of other groups."[7] Since humans propagate sexually, our species includes at a minimum men and women and moreover is *defined* with reference to sexual division according to humans' function in biological reproduction. Sigmund Freud famously explained that anatomy was destiny; many before and since have argued that this biological difference of sex tells us nearly everything we need to know about creatures I want to call "historical animals."[8] I think, however, that continuing differences in women's and men's histories are products of contentiously shared experience, a wide realm, more than narrowly mechanistic outcomes of bodily complementarity. There is far more to the enterprise of reproducing the species than the generation and gestation of viable human fetuses, a subject I'll be getting back to by and by.

Environmental historians, who wish to situate human thought and action in a world of other flora and fauna, have good reasons to try to understand humans as animals. But the biological concept of species, as we have just seen, is a rather dull categorical tool. At the same time it is also a complex, contradictory device. Even as biologists have put fruitful sexual congress at the heart of their professional understanding of human beings, biological science has perpetuated a naming practice that creates confusion, error, and inequality. I refer, of course, to the practice of referring to the human species as "man," or "mankind." I cannot do justice to the numerous elegant feminist critiques of the use of the male generic in English, so I refer you to a useful book first published in 1976, Casey Miller and Kate Swift's *Words and Women: New Language in New Times.* As Miller and Swift point out, citing the *Oxford English Dictionary,* in Old English the term *man* referred to individual persons of both sexes. The word *mankind* did not appear in Old English, first coming into usage around 1300. However, by the end of the first millennium after Christ, speakers of Old English had begun to use *man* in another sense, to distinguish a person of the male sex from one of the female sex. The older meaning, of course, persisted. As a consequence English would come to be a language in which no one could ever be truly sure when the words *man* and *men* meant males, and when they meant humans in general. By the eighteenth century, as Western Europeans and European Americans struggled over access to "the rights of man," defining the term had potentially immense political consequences. David Hume, who aimed for precision, referred in his 1752 *Political Discourses* to "all men, male and female." Alexander Pope, however, was a little less clear. His famous *Essay on Man,* published in 1733, admonished his friend Lord Bolingbroke to, "Know then thyself. . . . The proper study of mankind is man." Presumably he meant that all persons, male and female, should have self-understanding, but Pope left a puzzle behind in the essay, with a later reference to "thy dog, thy bottle, and thy wife."[9] When Thomas Jefferson wrote that "all men are created equal," he would make available a political argument for universal rights, an argument he by no means wished to extend to all humans, not even all males.[10]

Enlightenment science understood generic "man" as male, building on the classical tradition of seeing males as normative and females as deformed. The male generic has permeated not only western science but also common English usage. As a consequence both small children and scientists have tended not only to imagine that women's actions must be insignificant but moreover to assume "that all creatures are male unless they are known to be female." As

Miller and Swift noted, English speakers often refer to animals as "he," and "only ladybugs, cows, hens, and mother animals with their young are predictably referred to as *she*."[11]

The repercussions of speaking and thinking in male generics may sometimes be trivial, but they are also substantial. And science is rife with the male generic. Environmental historians rely on science as an analytical tool; they should be sensitive to the ways in which gender ideology constructs scientific knowledge. Biologists, for example, have shaped their assumptions about animal behavior, natural selection, and even genetics in conformity with the idea that males of a species are biologically normative, active, and essential and females are somehow auxiliary, or perhaps vehicular, even when the species cannot propagate itself without both.

This kind of thinking leads to some fairly weird and historically interesting science. My favorite recent example of such scientific work involved experiments by a team of researchers at the University of Sheffield in England, led by the globally eminent ornithologist Timothy R. Birkhead. Birkhead's group studied sperm morphology and sperm production in Australian zebra finches *(Taeniopygia guttata)*.[12] Whatever the scientific merits of studying sperm morphology, the larger purpose of these experiments was, I think, to say something not simply about zebra finch sperm or even sperm of various species but to speculate about "natural" sexual behavior in zebra finches and in animals in general, including the human. In our time, when sociobiology claims even the attention of historians, biological experiments bear heavy burdens of meaning. Indeed, as E. O. Wilson explains, in the sociobiologist's "macroscopic view the humanities and social sciences shrink to specialized branches of biology."[13]

Zebra finches are among those birds that were reputed to mate and rear young with one lifetime partner, a notion Birkhead and others have attributed to Charles Darwin's "touchingly naive" Victorian sexual mores.[14] Birkhead's Sheffield team, hailing from the other side of the sexual revolution, reported instead that such birds "occasionally enjoy sexual dalliances with other birds. Indeed, individual out-of-wedlock copulations have a higher fertilization rate than single mating efforts at home." To test this hypothesis, according to a summary account in *Science News*:

The team collected sperm by allowing male zebra finches to mate with a freeze-dried female equipped with an artificial sperm receptacle. When prevented from copulating for a week, a male would ejaculate several times into the dead female. Sperm from the second ejaculate moved at half the speed of sperm from the first go-around, a computerized sperm tracker revealed. Quantity decreased as well. . . . "The vagina is an incredibly hostile zone to sperm," so the faster they zip through, the better their chances of surviving, suggests Birkhead. . . . A male zebra finch has affairs only after he has recovered from copulating with his mate during her fertile period. As a result, he releases more sperm during one act of intercourse with his one-time lovers than with his regular gal, Birkhead says. Waiting until your own female is no longer fertile before you go looking for extra-pair copulations is part of the male strategy," he asserts.[15]

Now this experiment certainly raises some questions about thinking in male-generic terms when it comes to understanding the intimate lives of zebra finches. Do the nonfertile females have "affairs" too? (You may or may not buy the assumptions underlying this question at all. If you do, they do; see below.) Do they seek out as partners males who would rather copulate with living than dead specimens? Do the females who indulge in "one-night stands" with aging males suffer social stigma, or do they have no trouble attracting younger males with speedier sperm? An "artificial sperm receptacle" installed in a freeze-dried female zebra finch may be "an incredibly hostile environment," but is it really a "vagina"? Is it more hostile yet when such a receptacle is equipped with "a computerized sperm tracker"? And I wonder how, exactly, it is possible to see a male zebra finch's willingness to copulate (repeatedly) with a dead female as a strategy for reproductive success?

Clearly I envision a somewhat more active role for female zebra finches in the whole enterprise of sex and biological reproduction than such an experimental design can contemplate. And these days so does Professor Birkhead, who has spent endless hours watching and manipulating the matings of birds, including chickens, finches, sooty terns, rock ptarmigans, swallows, hawks, and spoonbills. Birkhead and Anders Pape Moller, his coauthor of the definitive work *Sperm Competition in Birds: Evolutionary Causes and Consequences* (1992), have devoted a lot of work quite recently to investigating "female control." As they explained in an article in *Animal Behaviour*, "At the time we were writing *Sperm Competition in Birds*, the idea of female control was still at an early stage. . . . The idea of female control has subsequently been explored more fully, both in terms of Behaviour . . . and physiology . . . and there is now some good evidence for it."[16]

It turns out that despite their many years of observing bird copulations, these two scientists had not until recently paid much attention to the fact that female birds had copulated with numbers of male birds in a dazzling array of settings and that after the acts, the females routinely ejected sperm from their

bodies. Not until 1992, in fact, did Birkhead and Moller burst the epistemological straitjacket of the generic male and begin to wonder to what those birds
were doing, and why it might matter.

And why did the scientists change their minds? As Birkhead and Moller
admitted, "After more careful research, and the occasional verbal batterings
from female colleagues, most behavioral ecologists have come to realise that
such notions [of male activity and female passivity] were founded on the
blinkered observations of male chauvinists. In reality, many female birds actually seek adulterous copulations. Far from being passive victims of adultery,
they are active and willing participants."[17]

I personally am not prepared to encumber zebra finches or other birds with
all the cultural baggage that comes along with adultery, but I think it is much
to Professor Birkhead's credit that he learned from those batterings from female colleagues and as a consequence has gone on to explore a rich, wide-open
new field for inquiry in his research specialty. How much more interesting
those long hours of sitting quietly in the copse must have become now that
both parties observed in the act of union may be presumed to have interests,
strategies, desires, and significance. Awareness of his own cultural "blinders,"
evidently, has transformed his work.

In recent years, environmental historians have also been self-critical about
the ways cultural notions inform seemingly scientific "observations" of nature.[18] Still, the man/nature formulation continues to pop up in the most
interesting places, for example, in a book much admired by environmental
historians, Michael Pollan's erudite and fetching *Second Nature: A Gardener's
Education*. Pollan is a beguiling writer and evidently a gifted gardener, but as I
read along in this book I was continually brought up short by his insistence on
referring to humans collectively as "man" and to nature in aggregate as "she."
In this formulation "man" tends to be purposeful but misguided, perpetually
intervening in processes "he" can't quite fathom and always creating consequences "he" didn't intend. "Nature," on the other hand, is energetic and
alluring, but utterly witless. *"Nature herself,"* Pollan writes, *"doesn't know
what's going to happen here.* Nature has no grand design. . . . chance events
can divert her course into an almost infinite number of different channels."[19]
Pollan is acutely aware that people who write about nature perforce use metaphors, some of which he finds misleading (nature as a "watch" or other machine), others "more apt" ("an organism or a stock exchange").[20] But for all
his sensitivity to ecological contingency and human folly, why is he so un-
selfconscious about reducing complex, diverse people to "man" and everything not "human" to a "her"? What are the implications of this rhetorical
choice? Man, in Pollan's world, is a deeply reflective Shandyan character, a less

dyspeptic Henry Adams seeking education but settling for experience, a Ricky Ricardo, shaking his head and muttering, "Lucy, Lucy, Lucy." Nature — earthworms, Norway pines, tomato plants, tornadoes, what have you — is in Pollan's world little more ultimately than a flighty dame, determined to seduce man with the promise of conquest but ultimately coy, elusive, and unreflective.

But "nature" is not one thing. Why shove zebra finches, saguaro cacti, tidal waves, uranium ore, and the AIDS virus into one vessel or, as engineers might put it, one "black box"? Such a formula is nowhere near adequate for the immense mission of environmental history.

Most environmental historians would, I think, find Pollan's personification of people as "man," and nature as "her," to be at least quaint or even embarrassing in the same way we are embarrassed when we hear a small boy tell his female classmate, "You can't play Little League. Girls aren't allowed." No, we want to say, that isn't polite. But in some senses, Pollan's overtly sexist language is preferable to the sex secret created when writers use seemingly neutral language while focusing almost exclusively on men's activities. There are a number of ways of measuring the extent to which environmental historians emphasize male humans' stories. We might look at the subjects and settings of environmental history studies, asking, for example, why scholars in the field have found forest fires more fascinating than cooking fires.[21] We might ask questions about analysis of data, as I shall presently. But another way to measure the disproportionate attention given to male activities in environmental history is to study the field's taxonomy. In field guides to birds, taxonomic distinctions are revealed in book indexes. So it is with environmental history.

Schoolmarm that I am, I recently investigated the taxonomy of environmental history by creating and performing a simple, even crude exercise in arithmetic. I looked at the indexes of seven important works in environmental history, all books I admire greatly, some of them written by contributors to this anthology. I counted up the number of male proper names and female proper names indexed. Then I calculated the percentage of male versus female names indexed. The results of this tabulation follow in Table 1.

It is possible to interpret these figures in a number of ways. First, note that indispensable works of environmental history have made specific reference to, almost exclusively, men. Carolyn Merchant's pathbreaking *Ecological Revolutions,* a book best known for the author's revealing use of gender as a category of analysis in environmental history, still takes note of strikingly few historical women. All these books claim to be about human beings' relations with nature, but their indices suggest that the humans being represented here are overwhelmingly male. On the other hand, Vera Norwood's *Made from This Earth* narrows its human subjects to "American women" — and comes

Table 1 Incidence of Male and Female Proper Names
in the Indexes of Environmental History Books

Author, Title	No. Male Names	No. Female Names	Male Names
De Buys, *Enchantment and Exploitation*	137	3	97.9
Worster, *Rivers of Empire*	313	13	96.0
Cronon, *Nature's Metropolis*	146	9	94.2
Rothman, *On Rims and Ridges*	272	24	91.2
[a]Merchant, *Ecological Revolutions*	173	25	87.4
Hoy, *Chasing Dirt*	113	102	52.6
Norwood, *Made from This Earth*	75	151	33.2

[a]Tabulations for this index exclude names of gods and goddesses.

closer, taxonomically anyhow, to telling a story with persons of both sexes in it; one-third of the people to whom Norwood refers are men. Suellen Hoy alone refers to roughly equal numbers of women and men, and my own estimate is that this taxonomic parity reflects her conscious and successful attempt to write a gender-balanced environmental history of cleanliness in the United States.

Perhaps the other environmental historians, whose works lean so much more heavily upon men's stories, have reached the conclusion that men's activities end up transforming "nature" more than women's. They have thus simply focused on what's important. I do not wish to argue either that men's actions are always different from women's or that we can make a simplistic correlation between the environmental impact of a group's actions and the size of its population — Americans, for example, are a minority of the earth's people but use most of its fossil fuels. But how can we *know* women's relative significance as agents of ecological transformation if we haven't consulted, in any serious way, their words and works? Without studying women's history, we will never know, for example, how women's actions, desires, and choices have shaped the world, including the things men have done, among them those things so ably and elegantly detailed in the works of environmental historians.

The idea that men have simply been more important environmental actors than women also begs the question of how we identify what constitutes "transformation" of nature. Building a dam or clear-cutting a forest obviously impress us as epic ecological events, but bigness is no guarantee of ecological significance, as Alfred Crosby's work on the role of viruses in ecological imperialism reminds us.[22] Mistaking size for significance also confuses the goal of documenting and interpreting the ways humans (or here, significant humans, i.e., men) have left a mark on nature with Worster's far more ambitious goal of describing *interactions between people and all the other kinds of things on earth.*

Another possibility is that environmental historians' sources limit their ability to see the significance of women's actions. Women's historians have long pointed out the ways traditional historical sources obscure women's lives. And given the sometimes terminal sanctions against speaking out, acting up, even eating "too much," women the world over have extended themselves, with dismaying success, to cover their own tracks. But this hasn't stopped women's historians from finding out a lot about women's past, and it shouldn't stop environmental historians either. Rivers and forest fires, woodchucks and white pine trees do not speak, but the literature of environmental history testifies eloquently to the presence and the significance of these mute entities. Women, unlike woodchucks, have the power of speech, but environmental historians have not listened very well.

At the risk of appearing downright waspish, I have to admit that there are times when the very best environmental histories almost foreground their silencing of women's history. As I was working my way through the index of Bill Cronon's splendid *Nature's Metropolis,* for example, I found an entry for one Patrick O'Leary. Turning to the text, I read about "the blaze that began in the barn behind Patrick O'Leary's cottage." This passive construction of the origins of the Great Chicago Fire of 1871 blandly skirts a story of human, more particularly, female agency familiar to every schoolchild in the land: "One dark night, when we were all in bed / Mrs. O'Leary left the lantern in the shed / And when the cow kicked it over, she winked her eye and said / There'll be a hot time in the old town tonight. . . . " Mrs. O'Leary does not make an appearance in Cronon's magisterial book. How can this be?

The *Oxford English Dictionary,* and Miller and Swift, remind us that "man" is sometimes human and sometimes male, and the confusion between the two constructions leads not only to further confusions but also contributes to social inequalities. But this linguistic heritage has spawned a further confusion, the "sex secret" of the literature of environmental history, in which all too often "human" *also* means "male." I want to stress here the political importance of this contest over what or who counts as "human" and remind you that just as science was launching its sustained takeoff into growth, the philosopher Mary Wollstonecraft was finding it impossible to convince most of the advanced thinkers of her day that women possessed enough of the stuff that made men naturally "human" to claim title to the Rights of Man. It is thus not surprising, as feminists from Wollstonecraft to Sherry Ortner and Carolyn Merchant have pointed out, to find human women perpetually slipping into the category of "nature," or to see the pervasiveness of gender as an organizing force in environmental thinking in the tradition of regarding "nature itself" as female and feminine.[23]

Numerous scholars have called attention to the identification of women with nature and of nature with women. I want to endorse the idea that women are, in crucial ways, embedded in nature: so are men. But in keeping with my waspish and pedantic desire to cavil over categories and claim the power of lecturing, I insist once again that women share with men the pernicious and noble attribute of being human. Thus, taking up Worster's charge to write a history that "deals with all the interactions people have had with nature in past times," I insist that environmental historians must own up to their sex secrets in order to begin to account for human activity, if nothing else.

And so I turn, as humans sometimes do, from sex to work. In 1979 feminist educator and organizer Judy Smith told a Missoula, Montana, audience that environmentalists needed to think more about the ways their attempts to advocate on nature's behalf might have consequences for women's work. In the years since Smith made this suggestion, environmental historians like Merchant, Vera Norwood, and Suellen Hoy have taken up the task of describing precisely those changes and consequences.[24] In 1995 Richard White echoed Smith's suggestion in *The Organic Machine,* writing that "one of the great shortcomings — intellectual and political — of modern environmentalism is its failure to grasp how human beings have historically known nature through work."[25] I agree wholeheartedly. Environmental history needs a broader, more nuanced, and far more gender-conscious understanding of work than the fundamentally Marxist formulation embraced by most scholars working in the field.

Here, at the risk of oversimplifying, I am forced to be brief and schematic. The environmental history I have read, from Donald Worster to cultural critic Mike Davis, conceptualizes work in relation to what Marx called "modes of production," one of which is, of course, capitalism. Most environmental historians treat the rise of capitalism as a process that rationalized, mechanized, and commodified work; alienated people from nature; transformed workers from producers into consumers; and in the process created distinct boundaries between work and leisure.

The following describes the capitalist transformation of work:

— rationalization
— mechanization
— commodification
— alienation from nature
— from production to consumption
— separation of work and leisure

However, feminist activists, labor historians, and feminist social scientists have demonstrated that industrialization and capitalist development led to the creation of all kinds of nonrationalized, nonmechanized, uncommodified (i.e., unpaid) productive work. As feminists have long noted, much of this work has been and remains women's work, often identified as "reproduction" or "consumption."[26] Following Anthony Giddens rather than Marx, I argue the need to abandon the distinction between production and reproduction, to instead see *all* human work as *action* entailing the *reproduction and transformation* of available rules and resources.[27] Those rules and resources may be as large and complex as the federal reserve banking system or as tiny as a lamp flame flickering in a shadowy cowshed.

Sometimes even spectacular ecological transformations may be traced back to mundane moments in women's history. Cronon's passing mention of Patrick O'Leary's shed inspired me to think about how to imagine an environmental history that includes women. Return with me to that dark night in 1871, when that horrible fire in the by then supposedly rationalized, mechanized, commodified city of Chicago was about to start. Experts disagree about what happened — most recently Chicago Title Insurance Company lawyer Richard F. Bales has used the techniques of a claims adjuster to cast doubt on Mrs. O'Leary's culpability — but contemporaries and modern schoolchildren swore that most people were in bed and that Mrs. O'Leary left a lantern in the shed, and the cow kicked it over, and the rest was history.[28]

What might Mrs. Catherine O'Leary have been doing in the shed long after everyone else was in bed? Evidently Catherine O'Leary kept five cows, earning money selling milk to families in her working-class Irish neighborhood. Cows need to be milked, or they get extremely uncomfortable.[29] If Catherine O'Leary was in the shed, she was presumably there to do that overdue milking. Women like her tended to have busy days, still doing their work long after dark. A cow in the city, a woman attending to her domestic chores late into the night. That night the men of the Chicago Board of Trade had left off dealing in mechanized rivers of grain they had never seen and had gone home to a dinner somebody else cooked, maybe read the evening paper while somebody else cleaned up, and then they stretched, yawned, and went up to bed. While they were enjoying a few hours of shut-eye, Catherine O'Leary's cows needed tending. The board of inquiry that investigated the fire exonerated both Mrs. O'Leary and her cow, a forgiving but, folklorically speaking, futile gesture.[30]

But let's not turn Mrs. O'Leary into a sentimental heroine of history. Try another story. We know that Catherine O'Leary kept cows in the city, but consider a wholly undocumented conjecture: Perhaps she wasn't always a responsible dairywoman. Maybe she didn't get around to milking that night because she got drunk in the morning and spent the whole day passed out in bed. Patrick, returning filthy and exhausted from his twelve-hour day, shook her awake and said to her, "That damnable cow is mooing her head off. What's the matter with you — didn't you milk her yet?" Mrs. O'Leary, bleary, staggered out to the shed with the lantern and then remembered she'd forgotten something in the house. But she left the lantern in the shed. Consider what happens when women *don't* do their work.

Ross Miller, who has examined the Great Chicago Fire as both an event in social history and a formative cultural myth, pointed out that in 1871, "In Chicago, a thriving cosmopolitan downtown still coexisted with Mrs. O'Leary's rural homestead."[31] You would probably get arrested for keeping a cow in Chicago today. But that doesn't mean that all work has been rationalized, mechanized, socialized, and commodified. Instead the gendered division of labor, symbolized by Catherine O'Leary in the shed, has structured the relation between nature, markets, and work to this very day. Even today domestic work remains productive, relatively unmechanized, unrationalized, generally uncommodified, connected to nature, often unseparated from leisure, and performed chiefly by women.

If as far as we know, women have not recently burned down any American cities (and that may simply reflect our ignorance rather than their actions), their domestic work remains ecologically transformative in ways that tend to be small and incremental rather than cataclysmic, easier to see in the aggregate than in the particular (and perhaps this, to be charitable, accounts in part for those skewed indices). Let me try to make a trivial part of that work visible by turning a personal anecdote into a story about environmental history. One fall day, I returned from the grocery store annoyed, as I often am, by the fact that getting food into our household had once again cost me an hour and a half of valuable writing time. As I began to unload the grocery bags from the car and ferry them into the house, I was reminded of that revolutionary moment, so brilliantly narrated by William Cronon, when grain dealers realized they could save endless money and labor by transporting wheat using steam-powered machines rather than human muscles and by storing grain in bins and mechanized grain elevators rather than sacks.[32]

Trudging back and forth from car to kitchen with my dozen bags, I began to wonder just how much freight I was carrying that day. And so, turning annoyance into science, I went into the bathroom, got the scale, and put it on the kitchen floor. Then I weighed those groceries sack by sack. That day's load, comprising most but by no means all of what I would purchase and carry during an average week's grocery shopping, weighed in at seventy-eight pounds.

Most weeks I end up at a grocery store four or five times because we've run out of milk or lettuce or coffee, or somebody has to take something to school for a class snack. I figure those extra trips add up, conservatively, to another twenty-five pounds of freight, but let's round off my weekly total to one hundred pounds of groceries for a family of four. Multiply that by fifty-two weeks per year, and you've got me carrying fifty-two hundred pounds of groceries a year. That doesn't seem too bad; only a bit over two and a half tons. But in the course of each shopping trip, I heft each item five times — from the shelf into the cart, from the cart onto the conveyer belt (then somebody else, a bagger, is paid to lift things twice, from the counter into bags and then into my cart), from the cart into the car, the car to the house, and once in the house to wherever constitutes being "put away" in my house. So it seems fair to me to multiply the total weekly weight of groceries by five in order to account for the number of times I lift and carry items to complete the job of "grocery shopping." Reckoned this way, I haul a total of twenty-six thousand pounds, or thirteen tons, of groceries a year before I've so much as opened a single can of tomatoes to make dinner.

Calculating the weight of my groceries may seem like a Taylorist exercise in whining; yes, it is that. And like much of arithmetic, this problem is pretty boring. But being tiresome doesn't rule it out as a description of a meaningful encounter with nature through work.[33] I have risked boring you in order to demystify the mingling of production and consumption, of work and leisure, of mechanization and labor power, of nature and culture: a woman shopper's encounter with gravity, a tomato's encounter with a can. This isn't very sexy stuff, but it is, I assure you, essential to reproducing human organisms. If I don't do this work, people in my house don't eat.

So, think: What percentage of that tonnage is packaging? Where does all that varied and hefty stuff comes from? Why do I choose to buy and carry and process and dispose of the particular things I do — Mexican tomatoes and South American ground beef, spaghetti from Italy and oranges from Florida, Corn Pops from Battle Creek and Budweiser from St. Louis? Pretty soon I am thinking about bulk marketing and recycling, about takeout fast food and home delivery pizza, about McDonald's hamburgers and the Amazon rain forest, about the global economy and ecology of eating in middle-class America today. Follow the trails of human encounters with nature outward, from the grocery bags in my kitchen, and I think you'll see some of the possibilities of women's environmental history.[34]

Imagine taking account of all the unpaid domestic work still done, mostly by women who also work in paid jobs, bringing home the bacon in more ways than one. How do they calculate their interests? To what extent has environmental history come to grips with the economic and ecological consequences of what they think and do? What new problems and challenges in environmental history does this kind of subject open up?

Let me make this unoriginal but still important point in the clearest possible terms. If environmental history is ever to come close to describing relations between humans and other things, it will have to look at, take seriously, and understand women's lives, and attitudes, and work, and the environmental consequences of what women do. Environmental history will have to try to see things from women's points of view.

Take Mrs. O'Leary and me, and the uncounted others whose work and thoughts couple together humans and other things. Given the choice of keeping a cow or circulating between my house and the supermarket, I emphatically prefer carting milk home from the store. For your information, a plastic gallon jug of milk weighs a bit more than seven pounds. We drink two gallons a week. I could, in the spirit of F. W. Taylor, save some work by buying powdered milk, but it just doesn't taste the same. I do seventy pounds of hauling each week, or 3,640 pounds each year, in milk alone, and I haven't even poured it on anyone's Cheerios yet. Or tried to detach four-day-old, formerly milk-soaked Cheerios from the underside of my daughter's chair, or thrown away the week-old, half-full milk glass my son left sitting by the heater in his room. Try to read forward and backward from these acts to see where they come from, why I do them, where they go.

These tedious domestic details are not, I know, heroic rendezvous between man and nature, dramas of dominance and submission, tragedies or triumphs. They are little didactic lessons, seemingly devoid of sex or secrecy, significant only because they are endlessly iterated and replicated. They are the acts that keep the species going, boring, idiotic, fascinating. I suppose they have at least those attributes in common with the kinds of sex secrets I haven't revealed in this essay.

I do not insist that all works of environmental history focus on women, or even that they must each and all do a very good job of accounting for the presence and significance of women. It is perfectly possible to write a decent book about men mostly, or even men only; many of the finest works of environmental history appear to be just such books. It is also quite possible to write books primarily or exclusively about women; I have read many such books and articles, and I commend them to environmental historians. I also know that women and men will often act in the *same* ways: we talk, we eat, we sleep, we are, together, historical animals. And we are, after all, far more like one another than are, say, hogs, diamonds, and rivers. Indeed, we should wonder if the only way to reduce the endless multiplicity of things to the unit "nature" is to pair that term with "man," an act of reduction arguably far loonier than leaving half of humanity out of environmental history.

But environmental history can no longer afford even the liability of concentrating so exclusively on male humans' interactions with nonhuman things. If ornithologists can learn from birds, historians can learn from ornithologists. Professor Timothy Birkhead has seen the exciting possibilities offered by believing that there might be two knowledgeable parties to the fleeting couplings in the barnyard and the bosky glen. Imagine with me, for a moment at least, an environmental history multiplied by the power of two, a history even richer, more complicated, and yes, more fertile than we have seen so far.

I would like to thank the participants in the New Mexico Environmental Symposium, who offered numerous comments on the paper I originally presented, along with those who have since read and carefully critiqued drafts of this article: Melissa Bokovoy, Nancy Langston, Les McFadden, Jane Slaughter, Kate Swift, Peter Swift, and Marsha Weisiger.

NOTES

1. Natalie Zemon Davis, "History's Two Bodies," *American Historical Review* 93, no. 1 (February 1988): 30.
2. Virginia Scharff, "An Earth of One's Own" (paper presented at the Organization of American Historians, Washington, D.C., March 1995, with comment by Dan Flores); see also Virginia Scharff, "Are Earth Girls Easy? Ecofeminism, Women's History, and Environmental History," *Journal of Women's History* 7, no. 2 (summer 1995): 164–75.
3. Donald Worster, ed., *The Ends of the Earth: Perspectives on Modern Environmental History* (Cambridge and New York: Cambridge University Press, 1988), vii.
4. See for example essays in *Uncommon Ground: Toward Reinventing Nature*, ed. William Cronon (New York: Norton, 1995).
5. Carolyn Merchant, *The Death of Nature: Women, Ecology, and the Scientific Revolution* (San Francisco: Harper & Row, 1980).
6. Merchant, *The Death of Nature*; Stephen Jay Gould, *The Mismeasure of Man* (New York: Norton, 1981); Evelyn Fox Keller, *Reflections on Gender and Science* (New Haven: Yale University Press, 1985) and *Secrets of Life, Secrets of Death:*

Essays on Language, Gender, and Science (London: Routledge, 1992); Donna Haraway, Primate Visions: Gender, Race and Nature in the World of Modern Science (New York: Routledge, 1989) and Simians, Cyborgs, and Women: The Reinvention of Nature (New York: Routledge, 1991); and Londa Schiebinger, Nature's Body, Nature's Mind: Gender in the Making of Modern Science (Boston, Beacon Press, 1993).

7. Webster's Third New International Dictionary of the English Language, Unabridged (Springfield, Mass.: G. C. Merriam, 1971), 2187.

8. See, for example, Edward Clarke, Sex and Education: A Fair Chance for Girls (Boston: Osgood and Company, 1873). For the best historical study of early-twentieth-century American scholarly attempts to combat the biases and consequences of biological determinist arguments about women's capacities, see Rosalind Rosenberg, Beyond Separate Spheres: Intellectual Roots of Modern Feminism (New Haven: Yale University Press, 1982). In this volume Max Oelschlaeger traces the philosophical roots of biologicalist arguments about sex and gender, while Dan Flores offers a contemporary sociobiological version of the biologicalist argument about sex.

9. Casey Miller and Kate Swift, Words and Women: New Language in New Times (New York: HarperCollins, 1991), 21–42.

10. On Jefferson's Declaration of Independence, see Garry Wills, Inventing America: Jefferson's Declaration of Independence (New York: Vintage, 1978).

11. Miller and Swift, Words and Women, 34–35.

12. More generally see T. R. Birkhead and A. P. Moller, Sperm Competition in Birds: Evolutionary Causes and Consequences (London: Academic Press, 1992).

13. The classic work on the topic is, of course, Edward O. Wilson, Sociobiology: The New Synthesis (Cambridge: Harvard University Press, 1975). Physiologist Jared Diamond, The Third Chimpanzee: The Evolution and Future of the Human Animal (New York: HarperPerennial, 1992), explains that some sociobiologists argue, "Our peculiar societies . . . have their closest parallels in colonies of seabirds" (p. 71). Feminists have of course practiced, interrogated, inveighed against, and historicized sociobiology; for a prescient critique see Ruth Herschberger, Adam's Rib (New York: Pellegrini and Cudahy, 1948), 68–84. See also Donna Haraway, Primate Visions and Simians, Cyborgs, and Women; Ruth Hubbard, The Politics of Women's Biology (New Brunswick: Rutgers University Press, 1990), 67–141; Susan Sperling, "Baboons with Briefcases vs. Langurs in Lipstick: Feminism and Functionalism in Primate Studies," in Gender at the Crossroads of Knowledge: Feminist Anthropology in the Postmodern Era, ed. Micaela di Leonardo (Berkeley: University of California Press, 1991), 204–34; and Evelyn Fox Keller, Secrets of Life, Secrets of Death, especially pp. 113–60.

14. Tim Birkhead and Anders Moller, "Faithless Females Seek Better Genes," New Scientist 135, no. 1828 (July 4, 1992): 34.

15. "Secret to Birds' Mating Score: Speedy Sperm," Science News 148 (October 7, 1995): 231.

16. Birkhead and Moller, "Faithless Females Seek Better Genes"; T. R. Birkhead, A. P. Moller, and W. J. Sutherland, "Why Do Females Make It So Difficult for Males to Fertilize Their Eggs?" Journal of Theoretical Biology 161 (1993): 51–60; Fiona M. Hunter, Marion Petrie, Merja Otronen, Tim Birkhead, and Anders Pape Moller,

"Why Do Females Copulate Repeatedly with One Male?" *Trends in Ecology and Evolution* 8 (1993): 21–26; T. R. Birkhead and A. P. Moller, "Extra-Pair Copulation and Extra-Pair Paternity in Birds," *Animal Behaviour* 49 (1995): 846–48.

17. Birkhead and Moller, "Faithless Females," 34.

18. Richard White, "Environmental History, Ecology and Meaning," *Journal of American History* 76 (1990): 1111–16; Richard White, "Discovering Nature in North America," *Journal of American History* 79 (1992): 874–91; William Cronon, "The Trouble with Wilderness; or, Getting Back to the Wrong Nature," in *Uncommon Ground.*

19. Michael Pollan, *Second Nature: A Gardener's Education* (New York: Atlantic Monthly Press, 1991), 183.

20. Ibid., 184.

21. Stephen Pyne, *Fire in America: A Cultural History of Wildland and Rural Fire* (Princeton: Princeton University Press, 1982).

22. Alfred Crosby, *The Columbian Exchange* (Westport, Conn.: Greenwood Press, 1972) and *Ecological Imperialism: The Biological Expansion of Europe, 900–1900* (Cambridge: Cambridge University Press, 1986).

23. Sherry Ortner, "Is Female to Male as Nature Is to Culture?" in *Woman, Culture, and Society,* ed. Michelle Zimbalist Rosaldo and Louise Lamphere (Stanford, Calif.: Stanford University Press, 1974), 66–87; Susan Griffin, *Woman and Nature: The Roaring Inside Her* (New York: Harper & Row, 1978); Carolyn Merchant, *The Death of Nature*; Chaia Heller, "For the Love of Nature: Ecology and the Cult of the Romantic," in *Ecofeminism: Women, Animals, Nature,* ed. Greta Gaard (Philadelphia: Temple University Press, 1993).

24. "Deciding What's Appropriate" (conference proceedings, University of Montana, Missoula, Montana, April 27–29, 1979), 5.

25. Richard White, *The Organic Machine* (New York: Hill & Wang, 1995), 2.

26. Raphael Samuel, "Workshop of the World: Steam Power and Hand Technology in Mid-Victorian Britain," History Workshop, 6–72; Wally Seccombe, "The Housewife and Her Labour Under Capitalism," *New Left Review* 83 (January–February 1974): 3–24; Pat Mainardi, "The Politics of Housework," in *Sisterhood Is Powerful: An Anthology of Writing from the Women's Liberation Movement,* ed. Robin Morgan (New York: Random, 1970), 447–54; "A Redstocking Sister" (Ellen Willis), "Consumerism and Women," in *Woman in Sexist Society: Studies in Power and Powerlessness,* ed. Vivian Gornick and Barbara K. Moran (New York: Signet, 1971), 658–64; Dorothy E. Smith, "A Sociology for Women," in *The Prism of Sex: Essays in the Sociology of Knowledge,* ed. Julia Sherman and Evelyn Beck (1978), 135–87; Heidi Hartmann, "The Unhappy Marriage of Marxism and Feminism: Towards a More Progressive Union," in *Women and Revolution: A Discussion of the Unhappy Marriage of Marxism and Feminism,* ed. Lydia Sargent (Boston: South End Press, 1981), 1–41; Laura Balbo, "The Servicing Work of Women and the Capitalist State," *Political Power and Social Theory* 3 (1982): 251–70; Susan Strasser, *Never Done: A History of American Housework* (New York, Pantheon, 1982); Nancy Hartsock, *Money, Sex and Power: Toward a Feminist Historical Materialism* (New York and London, Longman, 1983); and Ruth Schwartz Cowan, *More Work for Mother: The Ironies of Household Technology from the Open Hearth to the Microwave* (New York: Basic Books, 1983).

27. Anthony Giddens, *A Contemporary Critique of Historical Materialism* (New York: Macmillan, 1981).

28. Pam Belluck, "Barn Door Reopened on Fire After Legend Has Escaped," *New York Times,* 17 August, 1997.

29. Pam Belluck and Christine Meisner Rosen, *The Limits of Power: Great Fires and the Process of City Growth in America* (Cambridge: Cambridge University Press, 1988), 92.

30. Karen Sawislak, *Smoldering City: Chicago and the Great Fire* (Chicago: University of Chicago Press, 1995), 43–46.

31. Ross Miller, *American Apocalypse: The Great Fire and the Myth of Chicago* (Chicago: University of Chicago Press, 1990), 2.

32. Cronon, *Nature's Metropolis: Chicago and the Great West* (New York: W. W. Norton, 1991), 107–115.

33. As Richard White has pointed out regarding the Bonneville Power Agency, "The BPA is a large and boring agency, and boredom has served it well." *The Organic Machine,* 71.

34. A growing literature investigates this topic. See, for instance, Arlie Hochschild with Anne Machung, *The Second Shift* (New York: Avon, 1989); Warren J. Belasco, *Appetite for Change: How the Counterculture Took on the Food Industry, 1966–1988* (New York: Pantheon, 1989); and Marjorie L. DeVault, *Feeding the Family: The Social Organization of Caring as Gendered Work* (Chicago: University of Chicago Press, 1991).

CHAPTER THREE

CONSTRUCTING GENDER IN NATURE

*Bird Society Through the Eyes
of John Burroughs and
Florence Merriam Bailey*

Vera Norwood

In a recent essay on the contemporary development of the "ecological superman" Andrew Ross suggests that Steven Segale's character in his environmental adventure movie, *On Deadly Ground,* attempts to reconstruct a place in contemporary environmentalism for the classic man's man. Ross locates the historical precursors to this character in the "wilderness cults traditionally associated with the making of heroic, white, male identities: the frontiersman, the cowboy, the explorer, the pioneer settler."[1] Ross's essay, titled "The Great White Dude," appears in *Constructing Masculinity,* a collection of pieces, mostly by cultural critics of the postmodern school, considering how manliness and masculinity have been and continue to be performed in American culture. It is perhaps appropriate that one of the few essays in the collection to consider the representation of manhood among white men focuses on their role in environmental movements. Most histories of nature conservation and preservation movements in America have cast such men as the intellectual and political leaders of these initiatives.[2]

Yet except to note that this new "Eco-Man" can be lumped with explorers and frontiersmen, Ross does not probe the historical links between this specific version of male performance and the construction of nature. Nor does he do much to illuminate why women's roles in these narratives exist as a minor key, based in resistance to the violent, "muscular self-righteousness of the hardcore Earth First! genre of Eco-Man."[3] The essay begs the question of how the social construction of gender is implicated in what we find to value and preserve in nature.

Others in the postmodern camp are beginning to consider, however, just this issue of how we might address the connections between the invention of human nature and the invention of nature. Grappling with the problem of how to describe what exists "out there" prior to human constructions of realities we call "the world" or "nature," Katherine Hayles suggests we think of an unmediated "flux" with which humans are constantly interacting. Our construction of nature at any moment is made up of those aspects of the flux most meaningful to our circumstances, which are the "experiences of species-specific, culturally formed, and historically positioned actors." We interact with the world through embodiment, and "the precise conditions of our embodiment have everything to do with the nature of those interactions. The range and nature of sensory stimuli available to us, the contexts that affect how these stimuli achieve meaning, the habituated movements and postures we learn through culture and that are encoded for gender, ethnicity, and class—all affect how learning takes place and consequently how the world comes into being for us. To be incorporated within a different body would be to live in a different world."[4]

Hayles's model of human-nature interactions offers a theoretical model for testing the issue Andrew Ross raises, but fails to address how the construction of a natural manliness is tied to what men have selected from the flux and defined as "nature" and why (as Ross suggests has happened) such interaction places men at odds with women over both human gender roles and the "nature" of nature. To understand male and female ways of describing nature, then, we should consider the ways gender constructions have meant that men and women are embodied differently and thus live in different worlds.

The easiest way to go about testing Hayles's theory would be to look for men and women at radically opposite positions. This is essentially what Segale did in posing the female environmental voice in *On Deadly Ground* as an American Indian woman, which highlighted the differences but left open many questions about the origins of that difference. So much else is different in these individuals' lives that it would be difficult to posit the effect of gender on their perceptions of nature. The better approach might be to look for examples among men and women who share as closely as possible ethnic, class, educational, and regional experiences; who share a good deal of embodiment, except for gender. Since Ross suggests, and most historians agree, that the expansionary period of the late nineteenth century was a key period in the formation of the male character from which the Great White Dude proceeds, it also makes sense to look for case studies from that time period.

In 1886 John Burroughs, by then a respected American naturalist, conducted some birding excursions for the women students at Smith College at the invitation of Florence Merriam, who would go on to publish naturalist essays of her own and make a name for herself as an early female ornithologist. Burroughs and Merriam shared a general ethnic and class background, and both were well read in the natural history of their day and grounded their early studies of nature in the East. They shared an experience of nature that was based in familiar terrain around home or on recreational camping excursions that broke no new territory. From the flux of nature, both chose birds as the other natural beings most interesting to study.[5]

I selected the first published natural history essay collections of each for a close look at how their constructions of nature interacted with their sense of appropriate gender roles, with "human nature." John Burroughs published *Wake-Robin* in 1871 and Florence Merriam, who was inspired partly by *Wake-Robin*, published her first set of essays, *Birds Through an Opera Glass*, in 1889. Both books represent the nature constructions of young writers just beginning long careers in natural history, and both speak directly to the circumstances that led to their interest in nature. These two texts, then, may reveal something of the ways different embodiments led men and women of this class at this time to construct different natural worlds when they sauntered forth to study the plants and animals of their neighborhood.

Burroughs opens *Wake-Robin* in the posture of pursuit: "But what has interested me most in ornithology is the pursuit, the chase, the discovery; that part of it which is akin to hunting, fishing and wild sports."[6] *Wake-Robin* concludes on the same note as Burroughs elaborates that it is the closeness of the ornithological expedition to "sport" that makes it a worthy endeavor (202). The stance here is of a body free to range widely through space, adding new discoveries to our knowledge of nature, exhilarating in winning a competition in which bird specimens represent victory. The point is to play the role of the original explorer; that is the best way to know nature.

Burroughs writes here to other men. His essays are not only about birds but about how the study of birds in their habitat helps boys become men. The last essay in *Wake-Robin* tells of his own discovery of birds as a boy rambling the woods with his brothers. Other essays stress that boys need semiwild places, that they are particularly good at discovering nature's secrets, and that they and birds share a love for the "wildness and freedom of nature" (20). Boys become men when they are old enough to take up a gun and procure their first specimen. In only one brief phrase, when he notes that "any young person with health and enthusiasm has open to him or her the whole field," does Burroughs mention women. In the same passage he goes on to venture that once one has studied a bird's habits in the field, the culminating experience is to "shoot it (not ogle it with a glass), and compare with Audubon. In this way the feathered kingdom may be conquered" (205).

Although Burroughs hints that women might adopt this posture in nature, he did not really mean for women to take up the gun. His sedate birding ventures with the Smith women never led to such methods of collection. Women were of a gentler nature, as he notes at one point that only women can touch fragile hummingbird eggs without breaking them (116). As his comment about ogling with a glass demonstrates, however, he was incapable in 1871 of granting any authority to gentler forms of nature study.

How were women like Merriam to take their position in a world that the male ornithological establishment had constructed as about the chase and the original discovery? Fortuitously, perhaps, Florence Merriam had other inspirational resources besides Burroughs. Olive Thorne Miller had been publishing "ladies" bird studies since the 1870s and used her books specifically to encourage women to enter the field on their own terms. The solution such women came to entailed a posture in regard to nature that was quite different from that of Burroughs and his male colleagues.[7] In *Opera Glass*, Merriam does not position herself as an ornithologist (even though by the time she was writing her essays in the 1880s, she was well on her way to such a professional career). Nor does she attempt to take the role of sportsman. Addressing herself to "ladies" who find ornithology a "lion," she poses her nature essays as a "very gentle beast."[8] No real woman would view bird study as about the chase and capture.

Titling her collection *Birds Through an Opera Glass*, the posture Merriam adopts is of the unobtrusive watcher at the nest. With only a glass and a notebook, she argues that women may learn a great deal about birds. Where Burroughs posed observation of bird behavior as only a middle stop in the capture of a specimen, Merriam finds the moment at which the human watcher is able to closely observe the social life of birds the culminating event. Merriam is much less free to move through space and so does not have the option of seeking the all-encompassing collection of specimens that Burroughs's more aggressive form of study has for its goal. As she says, she must wait for what has "chanced to come before my opera-glass." But she turns what Burroughs would consider a constraint into a virtue. In her way of knowing the world, the best knowledge of nature comes from observation rather than capture. The ability to merge with the world is the best posture for achieving such knowledge: "I sit down in the grass, pull the timothy stems over my dress, make myself look as much as possible like a meadow, and keep one eye on the bobolinks" (30).

The masculine and feminine performances that Burroughs and Merriam adopt in their nature essays help structure different versions of nature as each selects what is important about birds from the flux. In the moments when he singles out behavior to study, Burroughs is primarily interested in male birds. Partly this focus is a function of the science itself, which based much of the classification and identification of birds on male coloration. Key to identifying a bird in the woods was also its song, an attribute more strongly evidenced by males than females. But Burroughs goes much further, using song as the key reason for any sympathy or interaction that might occur between humans and birds: "And what is a bird without its song? . . . It seems to me that I do not know a bird till I have heard its voice; then I come nearer it at once, and it possesses a human interest to me" (40). A birdsong is an art form on a par with human artistry: "The song of the hermit is in a higher key, and is more wild and ethereal. His instrument is a silver horn which he winds in the most solitary places. The song of the wood thrush is more golden and leisurely. Its tone comes near to that of some rare stringed instrument" (23).[9]

While Merriam discusses birdsong, it is not as central to her in explaining the reasons for selecting birds from nature's flux. Not surprisingly, perhaps, she is much more interested in domestic life. Where Burroughs finds supreme beauty and artistry in a male songster, Merriam locates it in the fit between a nesting bird and nature, in the creation of a perfect home: "The prettiest site of any I have ever known was in a sweetbrier bush on the edge of the garden. Here the little mother could be lulled into her noon-day nap by the droning of the bumble-bees buzzing about the garden. . . . Every breath of air brought her the perfume of the briar leaves, and when the pink buds unfolded she could tell off the days of her brooding by the petals that fluttered to the ground" (68). Obviously each has selected here experiences that in the human society of their time and place were tied to male and female roles—his stressing an elite, male art form and hers what was seen as the most fulfilling moment in a woman's reproductive life.

Burroughs and Merriam both study social interactions, between humans and birds and within bird communities. Here again, however, there are differences in what they pull from the flux as important. Merriam enjoys observing the social arrangements of different birds as they congregate around her feeders at home and even spends some time describing the cunning behavior of a pet crow as he establishes territory over the family dog. Most of her observations focus on nesting behaviors since "you never feel thoroughly acquainted with birds any more than with people until you see them in their homes" (50). When she discusses bird interactions with humans, she retains this emphasis on what might be called parlor behavior. She loves moments when she "converses" with a bird and deliberately seeks out more "trusting" birds for study. She is particularly pleased when she feels that a female bird understands and shares her interest in social life. Reporting on her happiness in making the acquaintance of a goldfinch family, she notes that "the mother-bird must have guessed my delight in her treasures, for she would sit quietly on a tree a few feet away with an air that said quite plainly, 'Aren't they dear little eggs? You can look at them just as long as you like'" (78).

Although she occasionally reports on aggressive or violent behaviors in bird society, Merriam does not emphasize these behaviors, nor does she often seek them out. Only once does she report deliberately intruding on a bird's domain with the intent of studying its behavior when threatened. And she quickly chastises herself for her slip. Standing between a mother redstart and one of her chicks in order to force her to display the trailing behavior that will draw away a predator, Merriam decides that the "love of knowledge gave little excuse for treating a poor little mother to such a scare" (184).

Burroughs positions himself as much more an aggressor in a natural world filled with violence and fear. While he mentions nesting behavior, he focuses on conflict. Very interested in birds of prey, he tries to decipher dominance hierarchies among the crows, hawks, kingbirds, and buzzards he observes in Washington, D.C. Unlike Merriam, he feels little guilt at instilling fear in birds, as when he sneaks up on a sleeping vireo: "When I reached out my hand and carefully closed it around the winged sleeper, its sudden terror and consternation almost paralyzed it" (209). His final objective is accurate identification of the birds studied; when in doubt, he shoots his prey and answers his questions. Even songbirds are not exempt from the pursuit; in fact, they hold the biggest mystery he would like to solve — how and why they perform. In an essay on the hermit thrush, whose song he calls a "hymn," Burroughs proceeds to understand the hymn by shooting one bird to discover how quickly another will take up its song and to study the instrument that makes the music: "I open his beak and find the inside yellow as gold. I was prepared to find it inlaid with pearls and diamonds, or to see an angel issue from it" (48).

Burroughs and Merriam look at nature through filters deriving from the natural science of the time, particularly in descriptions of physical evidences of adaptive coloration in birds. Burroughs also relies heavily on ideas about animal instinct to explain much of bird behavior. This is especially the case in his discussions of mating behaviors and propagation but also applies to dominance patterns. When trying to explain a specific behavior, he is most apt to use instinct as the cause and to generalize across individuals and species. Seeing birds as "generally regular in their habits and instincts," he is surprised by the rare occasions when their actions seem "as whimsical and capricious as superior beings'" (106).

Merriam selects much more learning and individuality in her depictions of bird life. She makes distinctions between the behavior of old and young birds: "The old chipping birds are very intelligent. The turn of the head and the quick glance from the eye show that their familiar bravery is due to no thoughtless confidence, but is based on keen observation and bird wit" (65). More than Burroughs, Merriam uses human referents to describe bird social behavior, suggesting both that she grants them more equality with humans and views them with much the same respect she bestows on her human neighbors. While Burroughs is interested in those aspects of bird social life that seem to compare to his own, his respect takes the form of dominance as he seeks to understand the mechanisms by which they come close to (but never reach) human behavior.

Proceeding from two different postures in nature, then, Burroughs and Merriam construct very different narratives about bird life. These differences extend into the crucial question of what we might learn about human nature from the study of nature. When speaking in general to their American readerships about what citizens might learn from nature, Burroughs and Merriam agree. Native birds teach us that nature supports a democratic, republican society. What the "natural" roles of men and women might be in creating such a society, however, is not much agreed on between Burroughs and Merriam.

Burroughs is very interested in what constitutes appropriate masculine performance among birds. Among his favorites are hawks. He specifically admires hawk behavior when under attack. Noting that the hawk's response to attack is to rise "to heights where the braggart is dazed and bewildered and loses his reckoning," he suggests that such an approach is "worthy of imitation" (34). Kingbirds, on the other hand, represent male "braggarts" and "cowards," and provide little of interest to humans (49). The freedom of male birds in general is much stressed in Burroughs. Male bluebirds, like their human counterparts, are "pioneers" in preceding females on the spring migration (191). Though Burroughs notes in passing that male birds will sit the nest as well as females, he does not see the males giving up much freedom to fatherhood. Beginning with a description of bluebird domestic arrangements, Burroughs goes on to generalize that among our most familiar birds "the male is the ornamental partner of the firm, and contributes little of the working capital" (194). Such behavior is, however, a useful adaptation. Following the received wisdom of the time on this issue, Burroughs argues that the male's song, bright colors, and freer movement in space serve to protect his family by making him more conspicuous than the female. Burroughs, then, creates a masculine society of courageous, creative, free souls, who in such behaviors support successful propagation of the species. It is hardly an accident that the human men he most admires (himself included) evidence similar behaviors as free-spirited sportsmen ranging the countryside.

Florence Merriam relegates most of the behaviors so valued by Burroughs to youthful males, who she presents often as young fops in need of discipline. Serious masculine performance is carried on by adult male birds who are seen as equal partners in the domestic round. While Burroughs devotes one rather uninterested sentence to the fact that male birds do sit the nest at times, Merriam devotes pages to various descriptions of male birds engaged in responsible parenting. The native robin, who is also cast as the good republican citizen, receives high praise, for example, for his "pluck and industry" in dutifully taking on "the burden of seeing three or four broods of bird children through all the dangers of cats, hawks, and first flights; keeping successive nestfuls of mouths supplied with worms all the summer through" (5–6).

While there is a sharp divergence between Merriam and Burroughs on appropriate masculine performance, on first glance it appears that they agree on female roles in nature (and human nature). Both agree that the most important female role is at the nest. Both suggest that females should maintain a serious demeanor. For Burroughs the female phoebe's "civil, neighborly ways" (4) are agreeably contrasted to the less acceptable behavior of the catbird, who is "a little too common" in her "loud and protracted singing" (26). Merriam agrees that the best females are "sensible, straightforward, industrious" (191). Her counterexamples are too forward, too taken with fashion, as with a robin who ornaments the outside of her otherwise unsuccessful nest with hen feathers: "Was this frivolous lady bird thinking so much of fashion and adornment she could spare no time on homely comfort?" (8)

Burroughs and Merriam do not agree, however, on the sources for female domestic roles or on their overall significance in bird lives. Drawing first from human social roles, Burroughs suggests that "there seems to be a system of Women's Rights prevailing among the birds" (102). Female birds (as female women) direct and organize the household while their "better-dressed" halves seek their "pleasure amid the branches" far away from the nest. As he does with social interactions in general, Burroughs locates the reasons for such female performance in adaptations directly tied to species survival: "I should say that the dull or neutral tints of the female [and her limited movements in space] were a provision of nature for her greater safety at all times, as her life is far more precious to the species than that of the male" (103). To Burroughs, male and female roles in society represent an example of biology as destiny.

As they do for himself and his male colleagues, gender roles in nature offer clear demarcations of male and female performance boundaries. "Women's Rights" in his mind concerns a version of the separate but equal approach, in which females get security and males get freedom. Florence Merriam took issue with this construction. First, she argued that beauty rests in the eye of the beholder—calling into question the argument about divisions between males and females on the basis of coloration. Commenting on the colors of red-winged blackbirds, Merriam notes that the contrasts may not be as great in the female as the male, but her colors are equally pleasing "and it is only a matter of taste if we do not admire her as much as her spouse" (91).

She goes on to link such "taste" directly to gender inequalities, connecting the scientific habit of naming birds by the male's coloration to "women's wrongs": "Like other ladies, the little feathered brides have to bear their husband's names, however inappropriate. What injustice! Here an innocent creature with olive-green back and yellowish throat has to go about all her days known as the black-throated blue warbler, just because that happens to describe the dress of her spouse!" (187). Merriam then castigates the "scientists who so ignore [bird] individuality" and concludes by noting that male warblers, who do not display "the slightest assumption of conjugal authority," offer a lesson to humans on this issue (188).

Embodied as a female in a time and among a class of women who were breaking down various social boundaries, Merriam looked at the flux of nature and pulled from it some lessons in how females might expand their lives outside the safety of the domestic round. Much as she loved the sight of a female bird on the nest, she also relished other roles females played and emphasized them in ways that suggested more flexibility in gender role divisions than Burroughs. In addition to her descriptions of males on the nest, she describes females foraging widely for food and both parents fiercely protecting young in highly visible ways. Countering instinct with intelligence, Merriam offers instances in which female birds break out of biological constraints. For example, she was most impressed with the behavior of a chestnut-sided warbler who understood that Merriam's presence constituted no threat and went about her business: "Fear seems to be an instinct, an inheritance with her, but her own confidence is strong enough to conquer it" (191).

The first works of Burroughs and Merriam, then, make a case for Hayles's contention that gender roles are one of the social variables critical to understanding how we construct nature and how nature is used to define human nature. While the initial posture of hunter or watcher at the nest is important to gender-role distinctions, these texts suggest that many other aspects of male/female embodiment play an important part as well in how nature is constructed. Merriam's focus on female birds, her emphasis on cooperative behaviors, her tendency to draw less divisive lines between animal and human, fit well with women's traditions in nature study. Likewise, Burroughs's focus on male birds, his emphasis on aggression, his reluctance to draw animal nature (couched as instinct) too close to human nature (couched as intelligence) are all aspects of nature study identified with the ways masculine culture has constructed nature.

Yet Burroughs holds an ambiguous position in the pantheon of the Great White Dudes of environmentalism. He is seen in environmental history as more marginal than such contemporaries as John Muir and Teddy Roosevelt. Even during his life, he was described by Teddy Roosevelt as the "methodist parson" of nature study.[10] This is because as well as his lack of interest in wilderness exploration and big game hunting, and his focus on the familiar landscapes close to home and neighborhood, he came in the 1880s to denounce many forms of hunting and collecting. In an essay on "Bird Enemies" in his 1886 publication, *Signs and Seasons,* Burroughs decried not only the bird destruction occurring at the hands of market hunters but also that done by amateur collectors who viewed birds as "trophies."[11] Such a change in values brought him much closer to ways of looking at nature rapidly identified with women as they moved into bird study in the 1870s and 1880s.

Ironically, the historical sense that Burroughs does not represent the most manly approaches to nature has served to mask the many other male-identified characteristics of his writing. The corollary to the hunt is the equally pervasive belief that nature, as represented in animals, is best defined in terms of instinct, which is often displayed in various aggressive behaviors. This was a view of nature that Burroughs embraced throughout his life, even more in his later life than in his youth. Burroughs's commitment to this version of nature informed the stance he took in regard to the nature fakers controversy in the early 1900s.[12] The battles between Burroughs and Roosevelt and Earnest Thompson Seton and William J. Long reflected in part the unsettled, divergent views at the time on how animal behavior should be described.[13] These were very much battles among elite men for the control of the dominant narrative about nature. Ultimately Burroughs represents the forces that won the contest, in the process narrowing both the generally acceptable versions of nature and masculinity in nature.

As the ethnologist Franz de Waal has recently lamented, this view of animal nature has become so reified that most men who study animals are incapable of seeing them as anything but instinctively battling for self-preservation and therefore have difficulty granting animals morality or sympathy. A number of female field-workers have argued that this model is a construction embedded in male ways of knowing nature.[14] In Burroughs's case, his reputation as the "methodist parson" of environmental history has led to a critical failure to understand his continued participation, even after he gave up the hunt, in the "man's man" view of nature. In an otherwise excellent study of Burroughs, Laurence Buell, for example, accepts Burroughs's contention that he did not personify birds, without considering that his constructions of bird behavior were heavily influenced by male scientific culture and represented a form of personification that has, until quite recently, become so habitual as to be invisible.[15] Burroughs's centrality to this male-identified, dominant construction of nature helps explain why the "methodist parson" continues to hold a prominent place in the environmental pantheon while so many of the women naturalists with whom he shared the stage have been ignored.

In light of this history, it is ironic that Andrew Ross surveys contemporary environmental movements and feels compelled to write an essay on masculinity and environmentalism that constitutes a defense of the virtues of the "Great White Dude" in his role as Steven Segale's "Eco-Man." Ross's essay is driven by his fear that the environmental movement of the 1990s is losing its virility to "the wussy New-Agers, the nerdy scientists, the celebrity fashion-plates, and the card-carrying social justice mavens."[16] One of the problems with Ross's reading of Segale's character in *On Deadly Ground* is that Ross separates this performance of masculinity from many of the institutions based in male culture. In particular, Ross assumes that "science" is some emasculated endeavor currently in need of a new hero, like Eco-Man, who can save its reputation among environmentalists. But much science has been itself deconstructed recently as a way of knowing the world deeply influenced by a version of masculinity based in dominance and control.[17] Likewise, Ross suggests that mainstream environmental activists need to be careful not to reject the "pragmatic satisfaction of kicking butt" (174) represented in Segale's character, as though many of the male leaders of these movements have not themselves engaged over the years in all sorts of confrontational strategies. The attitudes of the Great White Dude can be identified in much sociobiology, among field zoologists and anthropologists, and in the leaders of the Sierra Club and Wilderness Society. To call on the environmental movement to respond to the "evolutionary challenge" posed by the Great White Dude is to be ignorant of the ways the movement has been dominated by this version of masculinity for the most part since its inception.

A more fruitful approach to understanding how environmentalism might take an evolutionary step itself might be to probe more deeply, as Katherine

Hayles suggests, into the ways embodiment is implicated in the construction of nature and to question the privilege that has been granted to some embodied positions over others. The real evolutionary challenge posed at the moment to environmentalism is not the Eco-Man or the Great White Dude; the real challenge is to seriously consider how the construction of gender (for both men and women) is implicated in the construction of nature.

On this note, I find it interesting that some of our most important theorists currently attempting to reinvent nature have done so in ways that resonate very strongly with women's traditions in nature study. For example, although Katherine Hayles does not make note of her own position in her writings, her program shares the same ethic as that of her nineteenth-century sister, Florence Merriam. In her model for how humans might improve on their constructions of nature, Hayles suggests that we try to comprehend how other creatures experience nature. Doing so would also make sacrificing or exterminating other animals untenable because "it removes from the chorus of experience some of the voices articulating its richness and variety."[18] If Hayles really believes that our construction of nature is in part derived from gender-role constructions, she might well consider here how her program both reflects her own positionality and challenges traditions of nature study critically linked to the definition of masculinity.

Similarly, I have been struck by the turn among some men in our field away from the call of the wild and wilderness and to the virtues of familiar nature found in the landscapes of the particular and nearby, of home. I am thinking here of recent essays by Bill Cronon and Bill McKibben. In embracing the landscapes of Burroughs over those of John Muir, as McKibben expresses it, in embracing the "mild" over the "fierce," we will come into a more holistic experience of nature, one that will reground humans within, rather than outside, the natural world.[19] Unfortunately, while employing a view of nature that resonates strongly with women's traditions, neither essayist seems particularly cognizant of this issue. Worthy as the project of evolving beyond the wilderness cult may be, unless the men involved are able to incorporate a conscious gender-role analysis into the meaning of nature as "home," they may find that only the terrain changes; our sense of the human place in nature will remain uninterrogated.

NOTES

1. Andrew Ross, "The Great White Dude," in *Constructing Masculinity*, ed. Maurice Berger, Brian Wallis, Simon Watson (New York: Routledge, 1995), 174.

2. The standard history is Roderick Nash, *Wilderness and the American Mind* (New Haven: Yale University Press, 1967).

3. Ross, "The Great White Dude," 174.

4. Katherine Hayles, "Searching for Common Ground," in *Reinventing Nature? Responses to Postmodern Deconstruction*, ed. Michael E. Sale and Gary Lease (Washington, D.C., and Covelo, Calif.: Island Press, 1995), 50, 56.

5. Standard biographies of Burroughs and Merriam are Perry Westbrook, *John Burroughs* (New York: Twayne, 1974), and Harriet Kofalk, *No Woman Tenderfoot: Florence Merriam Bailey, Pioneer Naturalist* (College Station: Texas A&M University Press, 1989).

6. John Burroughs, preface to the first edition of *Wake-Robin* (Boston and New York: Houghton Mifflin: 1871). All further references are cited parenthetically in the text.

7. On American women's responses to nature, including this group of late-nineteenth-century birders, see Vera Norwood, *Made from This Earth: American Women and Nature* (Chapel Hill: University of North Carolina Press, 1993).

8. Florence A. Merriam, *Birds Through an Opera Glass* (Boston and New York: Houghton Mifflin, 1889), v. All further references are cited parenthetically in the text.

9. In later publications Burroughs compared birds and poets, finding similar creative wellsprings in the song of the bird and the words of the poet; Westbrook, *John Burroughs*, 31.

10. Bill McKibben, "The Call of the Not So Wild," *New York Review of Books*, 14 May 1992, 32.

11. Westbrook, *John Burroughs*, 83–84.

12. For more information see Ralph H. Lutts, *The Nature Fakers: Wildlife, Science, and Sediment* (Golden, Colo.: Fulcrum, 1990).

13. Burroughs's shift toward an increasingly skeptical regard for animal intelligence was fueled by the nature fakers battles of the early twentieth century and is documented in Ralph Lutts, *The Nature Fakers: Wildlife, Science and Sentiment* (Golden, Colo.: Fulcrum Pub., 1990). See also Lawrence Buell, *The Environmental Imagination: Thoreau, Nature Writing, and the Formation of American Culture* (Cambridge: Harvard University Press, 1995), 190–92.

14. Franz B. M. de Waal, *Good Natured: The Origins of Right and Wrong in Humans and Other Animals* (Cambridge: Harvard University Press, 1996). On the criticisms of gender bias in animal fieldwork, see Norwood, *Made from This Earth*, 209–60, and Donna Haraway, *Primate Visions: Gender, Race and Nature in the World of Modern Science* (New York: Routledge, 1989).

15. Buell in *The Environmental Imagination* (195–200) casts Burroughs as the representative of an emerging "modernist" camp in American nature writing (opposed to the "pietistic organicism" of Muir's animal tales) but does not consider the influence of Burrough's triumph in the nature fakers battles on twentieth-century field narratives or probe the sort of personification that goes on in such nature writing.

16. Ross, "The Great White Dude," 174.

17. Sandra Harding and Jean F. O'Barr, *Sex and Scientific Inquiry* (Chicago: University of Chicago Press, 1987), and Evelyn Fox Keller, *A Feeling for the Organ-*

ism: The Life and Work of Barbara McClintock (San Francisco: W. H. Freeman, 1983).

18. Hayles, "Searching for Common Ground," 58.

19. McKibben, "The Call of the Not So Wild," 33, and William Cronon, "The Problem of Wilderness," in *Uncommon Ground,* ed. William Cronon (New York: Norton, 1995).

CHAPTER FOUR

RE-PLACING HISTORY,
NATURALIZING CULTURE

Max Oelschlaeger

M y thesis draws from the work of the environmental humanists who argue that so long as history is defined apart from biophysical process, then dysfunctional relations between culture and nature will not only continue but likely worsen. Living in New Mexico, where the mountains, deserts, and rivers help constitute the woof and warp of daily life, there is a tendency to forget that western civilization frames nature as nothing more than raw material for economic appropriation.[1] Then again, despite the constant presence of place, New Mexicans tread with increasingly heavy ecological footprints on immediate and global environs. Whatever the traditions, today's New Mexico is increasingly dominated by what Robert Reich calls "the new symbolists," the economic movers and shakers, developers and entrepreneurs, who have brought prosperity and progress with them from Silicon Valley. The ruling elite is sustained by a discourse of power rooted in the foundational narratives of western civilization. All hail the "New World Order" and "Agenda 21."

Analyzed through an ecophilosophical approach, that discourse of power rests on the metaphysical separation of culture and nature, as manifest in the so-called great chain of being that places God our father over man, a male human made in the image of the divine spirit. Beneath God and man lies the material domain of woman and nature, subject to the controlling and organizing energy of the spirit, divine and masculine. The metaphysical antagonism institutionalized in the great chain of being colors the many different yet similar *concepts of human nature* that run through western culture, including *Homo religiosus, Homo sapiens,* and *Homo economicus.* For religious man, rational man, and economic man are first and foremost spiritual beings. (I use these three expressions as terms of art throughout the text.) And I emphasize the term *man,* since the *true nature* of human being in the western tradition is necessarily male and not female, an anthropology founded in the metaphysics that separates spirit from matter and elevates the former over the latter.

The devastating critiques of this discourse of power, such as those written by Gerda Lerner, Rosemary Ruether, and Susan Griffin, support this analysis. Lerner writes that the symbolic devaluing of women in relation to the divine becomes one of the two founding metaphors of western civilization. The other founding metaphor is supplied by Aristotelian philosophy, which assumes as a given that women are incomplete and damaged human beings of an entirely different order than men. It is with the creation of these two metaphorical constructs, which are built into the very foundations of the symbol systems of western civilization, that the subordination of women comes to be seen as "natural"; hence it becomes invisible. It is this that finally establishes patriarchy firmly as an actuality and as an ideology.[2]

Similarly Ruether deconstructs the metaphysics that places God and man over woman and nature. "Whereas ancient myth had seen the Gods and Goddesses as within the matrix of one physical-spiritual reality, male monotheism begins to split reality into a dualism of transcendent Spirit (mind, ego) and inferior and dependent physical nature."[3] Articulated through time, this initial division becomes the great chain of being, with God the father over all. God's creation is man, as exemplified by Adam, who is made in his image, and nature. Woman comes from Adam, God's first human creation. Not only does woman become secondary in relation to God, but woman also has only a negative rather than an affirmative definition. "Gender becomes a primary symbol for the dualism of transcendence and immanence, spirit and matter."[4] In Ruether's opinion the industrial revolution and the Enlightenment intensified the alienation of man from nature. "The nineteenth-century concept of 'progress' materialized the Judeo-Christian God concept. Males, identifying their egos with transcendent 'spirit,' made technology the project of progressive incarnation of transcendent 'spirit' into 'nature.' The eschatological project [of historical Christianity] became a historical project [of the industrial growth society]."[5]

Griffin's *Woman and Nature* also challenges the discourse of power. She is particularly effective at reminding readers of things outside time divided into events memorialized in history; that is, of our primordial relations to an earth unnamed, yet of whom we are made. "And we are nature," Griffin writes. "We are nature seeing nature. We are nature with a concept of nature. Nature weeping. Nature speaking of nature to nature."[6] The psychological-intellectual effect of Griffin's prose-poetry on readers is potent. Her text offers the reasoned argument and the affective impulse necessary to the intellectual and psychological effort required to resituate ourselves within the earth household. We come away from the printed page looking outward, suddenly finding ourselves in place, reconnected with biophysical process, with life in its chthonic ebbs and flows. According to her account, rational man conceals such realization through the scientific attitude of objectivity, by which a knowing and active scientific observer separates himself from and penetrates into a known and passive nature, thereby facilitating its domination.

HUMAN NATURE AS RATIONAL MAN

The foundational narratives for man as *Homo sapiens* are found in the texts of Greek rationalism, texts that constitute a virtual architectonic for the West. In the famous death scene sketched in the *Phaedo,* Socrates, having already pronounced that the true philosopher is always seeking death (the consummation of the marriage of spirit with the eternal and immutable realm of forms), directs his quietly weeping male friends to leave his presence and take refuge with the women. The normative masculine for Socrates is much like Monty Python's Black Knight in *In Search of the Holy Grail:* grievously damaged (i.e., having had his arms and legs severed from his body), he calls his opponent back to the contest, protesting that his injuries are mere flesh wounds. The archetypal male is purely rational, always in control of his lesser and baser feelings and emotions as well as of those who are incapable of rational control (that is, woman and nature).

Plato has on occasion been lionized as a defender of women, but on closer reading, his account of human nature is little different than Socrates'. The allegory of the cave in *The Republic* relentlessly reduces the natural world of sight and sound, of creatures and seasons, to nothing more than a veil of illusions that snares the unwary in the spell of becoming. Reality is being, and the knowledge of being is open to rational-masculine spirits able to cast off the appearances of the carnal, temporal world and contemplate truth, the eternal, immutable heaven of Platonic form. In the Platonic eschatology a few women, too, are allowed the opportunity to escape the realm of becoming, cast off the shackles of familial and household responsibilities, and become one of the guys.

Aristotle's most favorable interpretation of the possibility of female human being is that at best she might *glimpse,* though never fully know, the rational forms of things, thereby pulling back from the possibility that Plato "granted" woman the ability to emulate the rational intellect of man. Further, by her very nature woman is unfit to play any role in culture, including politics: Woman, Aristotle writes in *The Politics,* thy role is silence. Incredibly, Aristotle's biology denies the female any role in reproduction. Woman's role is nothing more than that of an empty vessel, her womb serving as a receptacle for sperm containing the male spirit that is the true source of life. (Robert Graves speculates that the rise of androcentrism was perhaps associated with the discovery of the male's role in procreation, something that was unknown until well after the Neolithic revolution. The appearance of writing and the interiorization of alphabetic literacy perhaps led to the theorizing of difference that Aristotle expresses: he was part of only the second generation of philosophers to write prose as we know it today.)

HUMAN NATURE AS RELIGIOUS MAN

Homo religiosus constitutes the second of three discourses that overdetermine western conceptions of human nature. These narratives first appear in the Pentateuch and then, much later, in the New Testament, itself profoundly influenced by Greek rationalism and alphabetic literacy. Gerda Lerner and Rosemary Ruether (as noted), and many other scholars, have commented on the profound ecosocial consequences of Judeo-Christian narrative. Theistic commentators, such as John Cobb, Jr., and Herman Daly, argue that Christianity has contributed to the anthropocentric exploitation of earth and more generally opposed attempts to reinterpret the meaning of human life in a time of ecosocial crisis. "It has generated suspicion of organismic views of human beings and of their communities, and fear that the distinctiveness of human beings, both their specialness of having been created *imago dei* and their radical sinfulness, which distinguishes them from the rest of creation, will be obscured" by the ecological reinterpretation of *Homo religiosus* (as defined by tradition).[7]

Let me very briefly consider two episodes from the long drama of religious man in the West, beginning with the beginning; that is, the Genesis story. Creation itself is ex nihilo, for Yahweh is a sky god, whose almighty spirit must be unencumbered by the limits of material being. Matter, in contrast to spirit, is always chaotic, incapable of forming itself. Similarly Adam and Eve are fallen, imperfect spiritual beings who, unlike Yahweh, are encumbered by the reality of flesh and carnal existence. Some two thousand years later Francis Bacon, aptly characterized as the man who saw through time, drew upon the architectonic resources of Judeo-Christian narrative to legitimate the coming of the modern age. For through scientific reason, rational man gained power: Knowledge is power, as Bacon succinctly put it. And through that power religious man might recover from his fallen state of sin and depravity, overcoming a hostile and alienated nature while creating a New Jerusalem on earth. Thus spirit might reign supreme once again over woman, who had caused man to fall into sin, and nature. Which is to say that western culture itself stands over and above matter; the palpable reality of flesh and nature are denied as mere appearance while the phantasmagorical, that is, a transcendental sky god and heaven, are claimed as reality.

HUMAN NATURE AS ECONOMIC MAN

Homo economicus is yet a third concept of human nature, rooted in metaphysical dualism and enshrined in the legitimating narratives of capitalism. (Though I do not discuss materialist interpretations here, many have taken this fork, most notably Marx and the neo-Marxists; as recent critics point out, nature fares little better at the hand of Marxist than capitalist ideology, for its discourse also harbors metaphysical dualism.) As economic man we are needy creatures, not entirely rational beings, ensnared in corporeal existence and the appetites and needs that flesh imposes. Again, like the Lone Ranger, reason rides to the rescue: for *Homo economicus* is most fundamentally a calculating, technological creature who bends the recalcitrant and niggardly earth to productive enterprise. Driven by self-interest, a concept rooted in metaphysical atomism, that is, the isolation of the human persona or psyche from any and all other influences, the market is ostensibly the rational institution by which each economic persona can achieve happiness, the psychic satisfaction of drowning need through the relentless increase of production and consumption. As envisioned by Adam Smith, the good society is built upon the foundation of reason that reveals to the rational mind the underlying economic laws of reality. By following reason, economic man overcomes the material insufficiency of the world and his nature: he becomes man at last, the master and possessor of nature now turned to its ultimate end, human satisfaction. Nature has an instrumental, or use value only, and only insofar as rational calculating man assigns that value.

HOW THE PAST OVERDETERMINES THE PRESENT

Each of these metaphysical vectors is alive and well, hiding itself in a thousand and one different ways in "ordinary life," in our everyday being, whether we live in Peoria or Tucumcari; Washington, D.C., or Albuquerque.[8] One among the many ways that *rational man* drives the course of history is in the dominating conception of environmentalism, the managing planet earth ideology grounded in the faith that the environmental engineer and planner are in control of the planet. "Agenda 21" and "Our Common Future" are little more than extensions of this ideology. Similarly *economic man* overdetermines the course of events: in a world already groaning under the travail of too many human beings with too many demands, the ideology of economic growth and development runs roughshod over countervailing discourses of ecological economics and psychology. And *religious man* haunts the human psyche: Ernst Becker's *The Denial of Death* is among the most incisive and accessible texts that explore the fundamental deformation of human being inherent in the psychological alienation from bodily being.

There is a peculiar irony, it seems to me, and genuine cause for alarm in fact that these dominant narratives of human nature that have overdetermined the human project now impel western culture toward a global ecocatastrophe. Yet it is possible that by revealing the concealed, by bringing the metaphysical discourse of separation to the level of conscious awareness, reconciliation might be achieved — or at least a project of reconciliation initiated. So long as human history is defined as occurring apart from nature, there can be no fundamental solutions to ecosocial crisis but only short-term palliatives and Band-Aids. Clearly *the idea of history* itself is a metaphysical creation: the ongoing course of history (deeds, events, as well as narratives) is driven by conceptions of human nature that deny the importance of corporeal being and biophysical processes. Our sense of human dignity, of the purpose and meaning of life, seems so profoundly caught up and entwined with a hidden metaphysic that no exit is possible. It seems we are caught between the proverbial rock and hard spot, for metaphysical dualism uncritically underlies historical discourse, yet remains, as all metaphysical concepts do, concealed and thus beyond the possibility of change.

Collectively *Homo sapiens, Homo religiosus,* and *Homo economicus* have isolated history within a cultural cocoon that defines human being and achievement apart from nature, from the earth and water, the sky and the soil. It is not surprising, then, that we teeter on the precipe of an anthropogenic mass extinction of life and global climate change. What is remarkable is that there are a few humans who have escaped the discourse of power, individuals who have raised voices of protest, challenged the dominant metaphysical scheme and ideas of human nature as these have coalesced in the idea of history.

Consider the works of the environmental historian and philosopher Carolyn Merchant and of Paul Shepard, a human ecologist. In a remarkable series of books published over the last twenty years, including *The Death of Nature: Woman, Ecology, and the Scientific Revolution; Ecological Revolutions: Nature, Gender and Science in New England;* and *Earthcare: Women and the Environment,* Merchant employs a feminist epistemology that challenges the theorizing of history as the project of man the rational animal. Merchant's histories are quite unlike those of the overwhelming majority of historians, who see in the ongoing course of civilization the triumph of man over an unruly nature inexorably bent to economic purpose. Instead she rereads the events of the last few hundred years and finds therein the roots of ecocrisis: history standing outside and above nature.

Merchant's work is not yet finished, but the direction in which she is headed is evident. Quite simply, she is re-placing culture and naturalizing culture. She argues, "To see nature as active is to recognize its formative role over geological and historical time. Only by according ecology a place in the narrative of history can nature and culture be seen as truly interactive."[9] Such a historiography resituates culture as a moment of nature, and history becomes a narrative of real people rooted in actual places, grappling with the realities of living on and with the land. Nature ceases being merely a theoretical object subsumed under the categories and within the algorithms of science and becomes a genuine subject or agent of change, including "surprises and catastrophes that cannot be predicted by linear equations and mechanistic descriptions."[10] And rational man is no longer the Cartesian master and possessor of nature, the dominator; rather humankind enters a new era grounded in the "concept of a partnership between people and nature." In this scheme culture is naturalized, that is, re-placed, re-situated, and re-contextualized. "A partnership relationship," Merchant contends, means that a

human community is in a dynamic relationship with a [more than human] . . . community. Each has power over the other. Nature, as a powerful, uncontrollable force, has the potential to destroy human lives and to continue to evolve and develop with or without human beings. Humans, who have the power to destroy nonhuman nature and potentially themselves through science and technology, must exercise care and restraint by allowing nature's beings the freedom to continue to exist, while still acting to fulfill basic human material and spiritual needs. An earthcare ethic . . . is generated by humans, but is enacted by listening to, hearing, and responding to the voice of nature.[11]

However radical Merchant's narratives, Paul Shepard's are equally so. Dave Foreman observes that Shepard is "the most important scholar of our time," suggesting that Nobel Prizes are not, unfortunately, given for this kind of "important scholarly" work.[12] What kind of intellectual endeavor is this? One that relentlessly calls into question the governing conceptions of human nature. In a remarkable series of books published over the last three decades, beginning with *Man in the Landscape: An Historic View of the Esthetics of Nature,* and including *The Tender Carnivore and the Sacred Game; The Sacred Paw: The Bear in Nature, Myth and Literature; Nature and Madness; Thinking Animals: Animals and the Development of Human Intelligence;* and his most recent work, *The Others: How Animals Made Us Human,* Shepard develops an analytically refined and empirically grounded argument that brings the concealed metaphysical grounds of the dominant conceptions of human nature into the open arena of scientific inquiry, intellectual criticism, and imaginative reinvention.

According to his account there can be no comprehension of the human project apart from biophysical process. Reason itself, the capital *R* reason of the rational man in control of himself and woman and nature, has no cogent explanation apart from the earth and the longueurs of biological and ecological time. "Like a ball at the top of a foundation," Shepard writes, "the human head pivots on its animal backbone, the mind a turning knot of thought and dream on the end of a liquid spear of living animals."[13] According to this analysis, the human mind "evolved among our primate ancestors as a part of an ecological heritage."[14] But bound up in narratives of history (itself a consequence of alphabetic literacy) we have forgotten the source and are blind to the continuing significance of animal nature within and to our own lives.

Shepard sounds a warning, arguing, "If culture is a characteristic of complex intelligence, then its rareness among animal species is perhaps a sign of its long-term fallibility."[15] Yet there is nonetheless hope, a hope rooted in what he terms a "post-historic primitivism."[16] Such a consciousness begins with a radical reconsideration of the idea of history itself. We must, Shepard writes,

stand apart from the conventions of history, even while using the record of the past, for the idea of history is itself a Western invention whose central theme is the rejection of habitat. It formulates experience outside of nature and tends to reduce place to . . . only a stage upon which the human drama is enacted. History conceives the past mainly in terms of biography and nations. It seeks causality in the conscious, spiritual, ambitious character of men and memorializes them in writing.[17]

THE ROLE OF THE ENVIRONMENTAL HUMANITIES IN RE-PLACING HISTORY

Imaginative thinkers such as Merchant and Shepard are, on my reading, underscoring, indeed insisting upon, a fundamental role for *the environmental humanities* in meeting the challenge of ecosocial crisis. They suggest that one goal of the environmental humanities, whether history or philosophy, anthropology or psychology, is to reconfigure the categories of nature, culture, and history and moreover enlarge their possibilities by freeing them from concepts of human nature grounded in a discourse of power. Such a project is pluralistic: there is neither a single discipline nor method nor art form that governs its direction. The environmental humanities range from disciplines and projects that are intensely theoretical to those that are concrete, from the wordplay of a *radical hermeneutics* that is "an attempt to stick with the original difficulty of life, and not to betray it with metaphysics," "a sustained attempt to write from below, without celestial transcendental justifications," or "an attempt to sway with the flow of physis without bailing out when the going gets rough, which is what that fateful *'meta-'* has always done,"[18] to the writing of *environmental historians* who actually build chthonic narratives, grounded in the ribs of soil and rock that hold the roots of culture. And the environmental humanities include the environmental social sciences, including sociology, economics, and anthropology, as well as environmental arts, architecture, and photography.

These efforts, viewed collaboratively and longitudinally, can help redirect humankind away from the precipe of ecocatastrophe and the "locust story" (that nature is nothing but a standing reserve) toward a sustainable world where humans think of themselves as members of the larger community of life. The work of the participants in the New Mexico Environmental Symposium can, and I would insist should, be read in this context.

Consider Vera Norwood's *Made from This Earth: American Women and Nature,* a subversive yet affirmative narrative that opens up new interpretive possibilities of North American environmentalism. Her narrative is, to say the least, an exposé that challenges metaphysical dualism by reconfiguring the role of women in conservation. She explains that *Made from This Earth* "centers around women in order to explore the question of how they perceive and act within the natural world. Obviously, American women who took part in nature study recognized that they entered terrain controlled by men. The male narrative defining the meaning of nature has formed a significant aspect of the context for their own efforts."[19] So far, so good. Here's the wild card. "I depart from traditional approaches to environmental history," she continues, "in situating that male narrative as a backdrop to women's efforts, and in questioning the extent to which women have found their nature values mirrored in those of their male colleagues."[20]

Norwood's treatment of Rachel Carson is a perfect illustration, since it goes to the heart of the question raised by the issue of gendered knowing. When Carson writes, "The 'control of nature' is a phrase conceived in arrogance, born of the Neanderthal age of biology and philosophy, when it was supposed that nature exists for the sake of man,"[21] she bearded the lion of rational man in his own den. On Norwood's reading, Carson upset the metaphysical apple-cart by arguing that "the model biology applied to nature was erroneous in positing the earth as a passive subject for man's probing and critical mind. The new ecology offered a competing paradigm that defined nature as active and responsive." Clearly Carson's argument shook the male-dominated scientific establishment: for metaphysics always serves as the hidden root of the discourse of power. "Carson's presentation of a scientific debate in a context critical not only of the chemicals but also of science itself," Norwood continues, "sparked many of the fires around *Silent Spring*. . . . To some men, that a woman not only entered their profession but also criticized it was unthinkable. They responded by appealing to the stereotype of women as incapable of true scientific understanding."[22]

Interesting, too, is the reality that Norwood's *Made from This Earth* is a narrative written from the margins, one that dis-covers the vital ongoing role that women have played and continue to play in the attempt to resolve the problematized relations between nature and culture. Her approach to history opens up a narrative space within which to tell a story that re-places culture and naturalizes history. Her pointed suggestion apropos of academic ecofeminism confirms the point. For academic ecofeminism, as with institutionalized philosophy more generally, is caught in the spell of metaphysics as it tries to explain and make clear and distinct the ideas that oppress women and nature. What academic ecofeminism has ignored, in its quest for theory, is the history of particular women in particular places who have made a difference. "Only by cultivating its own history, giving voice to women's collective work nurturing, preserving, and depicting the plants and animals of our home, will ecofeminism shape the answer to how women's culture can offer a better future."[23]

William deBuys's *Enchantment and Exploitation: The Life and Hard Times of a New Mexico Mountain Range* can also be read as part of the multivalent, pluralistic project that I immodestly outlined above for the environmental humanities. *Enchantment and Exploitation* will never challenge such tomes as Samuel Eliot Morrison's *The Oxford History of the American People* or Daniel Boorstein's *The Americans*. Indeed, in that context *Enchantment and Exploitation* is a tale of the losers rather than the winners of the historical dialectic. The text does not recount the story of great men who through the force of spirit overcame all natural obstacles in the way of human achievement but of successive generations of New Mexicans who were and continue to be shaped by place. He notes, "I realized that until I understood something of the influence of the land, I could not begin to understand the people whose lives and history bound them to it."[24] DeBuys's historiography goes beyond viewing the land as merely a challenge to the character of the men who tamed it. Rather, the land enters into the narrative of history as a fundamental player. "In studying place," he writes, "I have wanted to show that a society's relationship to the environment is reciprocal; it both changes the physical world and is changed by it. I have also attempted to show that the study of those changes can illuminate, in a most appropriate way, the main themes of the cultural history of New Mexico."[25]

Informed by the notion that history books begin and end and not the historical process itself, deBuys also envisions a role in his radical historiography that goes beyond mere antiquarian interest. For the effort of re-placing history and naturalizing culture outlines tomorrow's horizon and informs future possibilities. "The traditional cultures of the region," he writes, "are not mere aesthetic ornaments to lure tourists and stimulate the imagination. Like a rare plant or a unique ecosystem they are irreplaceable. Society needs to conserve them, both for the answers they give to the basic problems of existence and for the fresh new questions they pose about the proper relation of people to each other and to the land."[26]

Does deBuys here succumb to myopic romanticism? I think not. He realizes full well that ideas rooted in the particularities of the high alpine deserts and mountains of the Southwest are neither ecologically nor technologically failsafe, as the many ruins of failed civilizations dotted around New Mexico imply. But narratives of place offer a profound conceptual challenge to the dominant (Eurocentric) ideas that define human nature apart from place.

Finally, the *Idea of Wilderness* can be set in the same interpretive frame I've used with Norwood and deBuys.[27] Buried within the idea of wilderness we find its antipode — the idea of history. My wilderness tale begins with a speculative anthropology that discloses the outlines of oral culture and mimetic consciousness, where humankind lived on nature's terms, where there was no will to power, no rational man, no religious man, and no economic man. This era of the great hunt, an order that governed the human estate for more than two hundred thousand years, was left behind at the onset of the Neolithic food crisis. The agricultural revolution set in motion a rippling, interconnected skein of events that saw ancient peoples become increasingly adept at and aggressive in humanizing the land. Almost concomitantly they became aware of themselves as beings partially dependent upon yet distinct from nature. They devised increasingly abstract and complicated mythologies and theologies to account for their relation to, domination of, and separation from the natural world. These schemes recognized a limited mastery over the land through technology while preserving the idea that some forces were beyond human control; the land was increasingly conceptualized as divinely designed for human habitation, cultivation, and modification. Alphabetic literacy, once interiorized, led to the theorization and textual formalization of the legitimating ends of the West. Ultimately earth came to be conceived as valueless until humanized, no more than a standing reserve for the purposes of human appropriation. This tendency was reinforced by the first scientific revolution, which gave western culture the idea that man was the master and possessor of nature. Everything that followed in the wake of these changes, especially the last two, represented an unparalleled amplification of the exploitation of the land for narrowly human, utilitarian ends. The modern world in which we live has been built on this philosophy.

CONCLUSION

If western culture is overdetermined by the metaphysical narratives of the past, what, then, are the alternatives? Are we simply to collapse into the self-refuting skepticisms that either history is sound and fury signifying nothing or that we have reached the end of history or that history is nothing but the rationalizing stories written by the victors? Or can reinterpreted categories of nature and history, rooted in the particularities of place, actually find relevance in the context of environmental issues, policies, and projects, such as water resources in New Mexico? I think the latter is a viable possibility.

Even as the new symbolists legitimate the unrestrained mining of the fossil waters underlying Albuquerque, countervailing discourses, grounded in a sense of history tied to place and an awareness of a culture that is naturalized, have appeared. Consider an example from *Intel Inside New Mexico: A Case Study of Environmental and Economic Injustice:* "Although many developers and politicians have big plans for the growth of Albuquerque, the metropolitan area's expansion is held in check by its geographic location."[28] And, the report continues, the rush to progress is also challenged by the very existence of the people who have traditionally lived on these lands. Yet these people, future generations of New Mexicans, and all the flora and fauna dependent on water, are forgotten, overwhelmed beneath the rationalizing power of benefit-cost analysis. "The Pueblo of Sandia's aquifer is now being pulled in every way from beneath their feet; towards the wealthy developments of the northeast heights; towards the west side for Intel and the expansion of the Silicon Mesa; towards the huge electronics factories to the south; and to the north a factory owned by Centex pumps large amounts of water to produce wall board. Sandia, along with all of the other Pueblos, may be further impacted as Intel and industrial water users continue to buy water rights in New Mexico."[29]

For those conversant with the remarkable environmental histories dealing with water resources in the arid West, such as Donald Worster's *Rivers of Empire* and Marc Reisner's *Cadillac Desert,* there is little surprise in this turn of events. "We set out to make the future of the American West secure," Reisner concludes; "what we really did was make ourselves rich and our descendants insecure."[30] And even then, all have not participated in the short-term windfall of profits reaped from water. Whatever economic benefits have flowed to New Mexicans, as some of them realized the American dream of success for the first time in their lives, the river of profits has mainly flowed back to the centers of imperial power: Los Angeles, San Francisco, Chicago, and New York. And when the water is gone, so too will the jobs disappear, as the empire moves its fabrication plants to greener pastures. Taken seriously, then, the environmental humanities offer some hope of overcoming the criticism that philosophers specifically, and intellectuals more generally, have long speculated about the world but failed to change it.

NOTES

1. For a succinct definition see Neil Evernden, "Resourcism," in *Conservation and Environmentalism: An Encyclopedia,* ed. Robert Paehlke (New York: Garland, 1995).
2. Gerda Lerner, *The Creation of Patriarchy* (New York: Oxford University Press, 1986).
3. Rosemary Radford Ruether, *Gaia and God: An Ecofeminist Theology of Earth Healing* (San Francisco: Harper San Francisco, 1992), 54.
4. Ruether, *Gaia and God,* 54.
5. Rosemary Radford Ruether, *New Woman, New Earth: Sexist Ideologies and Human Liberation* (San Francisco: Harper & Row, 1975), 194.

6. Susan Griffin, *Woman and Nature: The Roaring Inside Her* (New York: Harper & Row, 1978), 226.

7. Herman E. Daly and John B. Cobb, Jr., *For the Common Good: Redirecting the Economy Toward Community, the Environment, and a Sustainable Future* (Boston: Beacon Press, 1989), 376–77.

8. On narrative and human agency see Charles Taylor, *Sources of the Self* (Cambridge: Harvard University Press, 1989).

9. Carolyn Merchant, *Ecological Revolutions: Nature, Gender, and Science in New England* (Chapel Hill: University of North Carolina Press, 1989), 28.

10. Merchant, *Ecological Revolutions*, 268.

11. Carolyn Merchant, *Earthcare: Women and the Environment* (New York: Routledge, 1996), xix.

12. Dave Foreman, quoted in *The Company of Others: Essays on Paul Shepard*, ed. Max Oelschlaeger (Durango, Colo.: Kivaki Press, 1995).

13. Paul Shepard, *Thinking Animals: Animals and the Development of Human Intelligence* (New York: Viking Press, 1978), 261.

14. Paul Shepard, *The Others: How Animals Made Us Human* (Washington, D.C.: Island Press/Shearwater Books, 1995), 15.

15. Shepard, *The Others*, 17.

16. See Paul Shepard, "Post-historic Primitivism," in *The Wilderness Condition: Essays on Environment and Civilization*, ed. Max Oelschlaeger (San Francisco: Sierra Club Books, 1992).

17. Paul Shepard, *Nature and Madness* (San Francisco: Sierra Club Books, 1982), 47.

18. John D. Caputo, *Radical Hermeneutics: Repetition, Deconstruction, and the Hermeneutic Project* (Bloomington: Indiana University Press, 1987), 1, 273.

19. Vera Norwood, *Made from This Earth: American Women and Nature* (Chapel Hill: University of North Carolina Press, 1993), xiv–xv.

20. Norwood, *Made from This Earth*, xv.

21. Rachel Carson, *Silent Spring* (Greenwich: Fawcett, 1962), 261.

22. Norwood, *Made from This Earth*, 169.

23. Ibid., 284.

24. William deBuys, *Enchantment and Exploitation: The Life and Hard Times of a New Mexico Mountain Range* (Albuquerque: University of New Mexico Press, 1985), 8.

25. Ibid., 8.

26. Ibid., 319.

27. Max Oelschlaeger, *The Idea of Wilderness: From Prehistory to the Age of Ecology* (New Haven: Yale University Press, 1991).

28. *Intel Inside New Mexico: A Case Study of Environmental and Economic Injustice* (Albuquerque: Southwest Organizing Project, 1995), 64.

29. Ibid., 64–65.

30. Marc Reisner, *Cadillac Desert: The American West and Its Disappearing Water* (New York: Viking Press, 1986), 486.

PART II

Human/Nature Stories

W hile the essays in the first section represented an attempt to examine the concept of human nature against the larger backdrop of science and culture, in this second section the authors illustrate how assumptions of human nature manifest themselves in American culture in general and the politics of environmentalism in particular. William deBuys, John Herron, Paul Hirt, and Andrew Kirk each write about how different cultural groups construct stories about nature, people, and human nature. Among the questions posed by these authors are the following: Despite the evidence against a universal human nature, why does it continue to influence the stories we tell about the environment? In what ways have assumptions about human nature shaped environmental politics and advocacy? How do the connections between humans and nature influence our understanding of native cultures? And finally, what role do ideas of human nature play in the politics of historical narrative?

In his essay "St. Francis in the Low Post," William deBuys nicely summarizes the problems with the idea of human nature while examining scientific attempts to understand human behavior and the persistence of the idea of human nature in guiding this quest. Focusing on the notion of "sustainability," deBuys explores the variety of ways that different cultures tell stories about their relationship with nature. Humans are gambling with their use of the planet, deBuys argues, and understanding the narratives that describe this risk is key to comprehending the consequences of future human adaptability to the land.

Using wildfire as a window into the exploration of the relationship between humans, nature, and human nature, John Herron examines fire not only as a powerful ecological event but also as a fundamental element of human culture. By searching for a better understanding of the intimate cultural connection between humans and the nonhuman world, this essay focuses on how society, specifically Native American society, has used fire to constantly shape and reshape their world. This ability to mold nature and, importantly, our perceptions of this behavior, speaks to the enduring complexity of our notions of human nature.

Andrew Kirk's essay is a brief meditation on the Conservation Library of Denver, Colorado, that raises and tries to answer a set of questions about the efforts of a small yet influential group of environmental thinkers to construct a monument to themselves and their philosophy and the ways these efforts reflect some basic assumptions about nature and human nature in environmental discourse. The story of the Conservation Library and the effort to preserve a particular vision of the environment in space and artifacts, Kirk argues, reveals assumptions about human nature and shows how those assumptions inform both environmental advocacy and environmental history.

Finally, Paul Hirt looks at the ways environmental historians construct and people their narratives. Hirt's analysis of environmental stories demonstrates that authors often reveal assumptions about human nature by the types of character traits they identify in their subjects. If humans are storytelling animals, as most of our essayists assert, then understanding narrative and narrative strategies is one key to understanding perceptions of human nature. Hirt's thorough taxonomy of narrative tactics helps underscore the ways that ideas of human nature operate without acknowledgment from the author.

CHAPTER FIVE

ST. FRANCIS IN THE LOW POST, OR, SUSTAINABLE DEVELOPMENT AND THE NATURE OF ENVIRONMENTAL STORIES

William deBuys

The term *human nature* harkens to an older, more self-assured day than ours. A quick check of Bartlett's *Familiar Quotations* confirms that the idea of an essential humanness has inspired many a memorable statement, nearly all of which, as recorded in that collection, were pronounced more than a century ago. Tacitus, Macaulay, Wordsworth, Hawthorne, Lincoln, Fielding, Emily Dickinson, Herbert Spencer, Henry Adams, and many others have weighed in on the subject, but by the reckoning of John Bartlett's editorial successors, all sources notable and quotable since then, with the quizzical exception of Ogden Nash, have weighed out. The concept of human nature may not have long to wait before it joins "natural philosophy" and the diagnostic typology of the "moral imbecile" in the Old Notions Wing of the Museum of Intellectual Fashion. Perhaps it is already there.

A history of the decline of human nature as an organizing concept in the study of humankind deserves to be written. It seems likely that such a history would show that Darwin cracked the concept's foundation, after which anthropologists, ethnologists, and psychologists disassembled it from roof peak to stem wall. A century and a half of social science has shown that for every quality assumed integral to human nature, there exists a tribe, band, or culture group that embraces its opposite as a core characteristic. Acquisitiveness, belligerence, sexual jealousy, curiosity — somewhere between the ice caps there live, or have lived, people whose "nature" leads them to embrace and embody an opposite character. Indeed, if we were to conceive an Olympics of human diversity, we might imagine a championship basketball competition with a starting five, on one side, of Emily Dickinson, Niels Bohr, Siddhārtha, Pol Pot, and Nanook of the North, tipping it off against Francis of Assisi, Gauguin, Ma Rainey, Nefertiti, and Ishi. Timothy McVeigh and Pericles could be the refs.

Modern biology has done for human nature what particle physics did for the atom: it has shown that "things" once thought indivisible in fact have smaller constituents. Endorphins, for instance—together with the putatively obligate quest for them—have been sheared from the ontological human core like up quarks from a proton. But our success at dissection does not necessarily advance us in conceiving of the whole. A picture of what these constituent parts mean, taken together, eludes us, today perhaps more than ever.

As hard as it might be to postulate one human nature that fits all, many of us intuitively believe that it must exist, if only in our minds, and that it is important to environmental history. As Art McEvoy has pointed out, Garret Hardin's tragedy of the commons would not be half as tragic if Hardin traded his Hobbesian model of human behavior for one in which humans actually talked to each other.[1] And one may usefully argue that different conceptions of human nature (or at least of American cultural nature) underlie the respective models of western settlement forwarded by Frederick Jackson Turner, Walter Webb, and contemporary revisionists.

One also sees the influence of various conceptions of human nature in current debate over natural resource issues. One cadre of policy specialists in particular—libertarian resource economists—depend on a singular assessment of humanness.[2] Their core argument is that by allowing markets to function freely, we can solve or improve most problems of resource allocation and management—this because, in their view, humankind is more *Homo economicus* than *sapiens,* or anything else. *Economicus* was born to do—and only do—what is in his immediate material interest, which is to seek satisfaction. If pricing operates freely (an oxymoronic concept at one level, but let us not pause), then prices will reflect true costs and real values, and the laws of supply and demand, unfettered, will maintain economic—and environmental—order. This is a singular and quite likely ethnocentric view, but let us not be diverted into debating its merits or lack of them.[3]

My point is that our visions of human nature do indeed matter, notwithstanding that when we peer into the laboratories of biologists to glimpse our constituent parts, we are at pains to behold what we had hoped to see. We see endocrine function; we see neural networks; we see brains and glands and cardiac muscle. But try as we might, we see no hearts or souls or natures, nor do we hear about them. Even our most basic questions go unanswered: What is consciousness? Why do we sleep? Why do we dream?

But we are not entirely bereft of guidance. Down the hall is the cognition lab. When we study how we learn, we learn that all humans tell stories. Here is something to hold on to, something, perhaps, in our natures. The stories may not be intelligible across cultures, as the work of Somerset Maugham may not mean much in the Guinean interior and the dream epics of the Mohave might fail to survive translation in Hoboken, but all are stories nonetheless. The compulsive telling of stories may be humankind's most pervasive, equal-opportunity characteristic. We use stories to learn and to teach, to explain, to amuse, to orient ourselves in the cosmos. All of us: men and women; pre-, proto-, post-, and pure industrial economic actors; workers and owners; the melanin-challenged together with the genetically tanned; all God's children and the devil's disciples, too, seem to have stories to tell, and to tell them incessantly.

Storytelling even prevails in precincts where quantitative data might be thought to dominate discussions and decision making. Alan Greenspan, the chairman of the Federal Reserve Board, testified to Congress in 1994, for instance, that in attempting to divine where inflation might be heading, he relies not just on "hard" economic data but on "detailed readings of firm behavior." Members of Congress scratched their heads in puzzlement until they realized what this last concept represented: Chairman Greenspan was talking about stories.[4]

In environmental history, as in every arena of human endeavor, we express our insights and our understandings through stories, and some of these have exerted profound influence on the relationship of societies to their environment. George Perkins Marsh, for instance, told the same story over and over in *Man and Nature:* namely that waste, neglect, and human misuse of forests and watersheds were destroying the capacity of settled lands to support human occupation. The moral of the story was crystal-clear: society must conserve resources or face decline, and in this country, by the turn of the century, people who called themselves *Progressives* had begun to translate that imperative into action.

Marsh had written a kind of environmental Genesis, and the Progressives elaborated Marsh's core message with their own equivalents of Exodus, Deuteronomy, and the books of several prophets—among them Pinchot, Roosevelt, Merriam, and McGee. Their collective testament promised salvation if only land were saved for managed use and used expertly. Meanwhile a second story circulated in counterpoint to the first, and from the Book of John (Muir, that is) we learn that the central theme of this new testament was that wild lands should be saved not *for* but *from* use. Roderick Nash annotates this and successive gospels in *Wilderness and the American Mind*, which is perhaps as close as the literature of environmental scholarship has come to old-fashioned triumphalism. Nash's story is one of hard-won but steady gains, culminating in passage of the 1964 Wilderness Act, and it remains a core text of the environmental movement, which continues to press for wilderness and for protective management of any land that might be said to be wild or natural (although both of those terms are notoriously hard to define).

But neither circumstances nor stories remain the same for long. In recent years The Nature Conservancy has waged an ambitious fund-raising and land protection effort, which it calls its Last Best Places campaign. The name expresses a fundamental reality with which the land-conserving wing of the environmental movement has been obliged to cope: unprotected places that are glamorously big and ecologically intact — at least in the United States — are increasingly rare. Most large ecosystem complexes that are arguably wild or natural have either already received a measure of formal protection or have become so altered or otherwise subject to intensive human use that protection — in the sense of setting them "aside" — is no longer an option. This reality alone would eventually prompt revision of the story of land preservation, but other, equally important factors have hastened the generation of a new organizing concept for environmentalism. Let me mention two of them:

— Increasing acknowledgment within the scientific community and elsewhere that few existing protected areas, be they wilderness areas or national parks, are large enough by themselves to maintain ecological diversity or landscape integrity. This means that management of lands adjacent to protected reservations must be integrated with the reservations' management if the environmental values of the whole are to be maintained. These adjacent lands, meanwhile, usually support a range of human uses.

— Public frustration with "command and control" approaches to environmental regulation. The perception that regulatory decisions may be arbitrary or punitive and that environmentalists, through legal activism and judicial and administrative appeals, are producing "gridlock" in the management of public lands and natural resources has led to renewed cries, from both environmentalists and their critics, for approaches to conservation that produce consensus, cooperation, and tangible results.

Taken together, these tensions represent conditions that a new "story" for American environmentalism must address. To generate that story, American environmentalism seems to be borrowing strongly from the international arena, adopting for its own a story known, at least for now, by the title "sustainable development." The definition of the term that is most widely—but by no means universally—accepted is that provided by the World Commission on Environment and Development in 1987. It describes sustainable development as "development that meets the needs of the present generation without compromising the ability of future generations to meet their own needs."[5] Acceptance of such a goal—which is to say, acknowledgment that such a story is valid—is an act of optimism. By it one asserts that economic use of environmental resources can be made compatible with good stewardship of them.

Clearly, say advocates of sustainable development, humankind must make usufruct of the planet; the challenge of survival is to do so sustainably. Fair enough. But the question we are obliged to try to answer is whether the story that we tell ourselves under the title of sustainable development is true, or at least true enough that it can guide us toward the cherished if linguistically unlovely goal of "sustainability." We must consider whether the story might be a fraud, a lullaby we sing when we wake with fright on our journey into the heart of environmental darkness and glimpse the horror of Malthusian depletion and degradation. To return to the biblical metaphor introduced a few pages back, we must ask if sustainable development is a new testament or only an apocrypha, wherein resides a further story of apocalypse.

It is only human nature, perhaps, that we organize our lives and express our values through stories, and perhaps it is also only human nature that our stories should, on the whole, be hopeful. Despair, after all, rarely inspires the resolve necessary for solving difficult problems. But questions attendant to "sustainable development" merit close examination and deserve the interest and energies of environmental historians.

Sustainable development is certainly not a new idea, and examples of success in this field, while not abounding, certainly exist, including here in the Southwest. Take, for example, the pueblo of Acoma, which dates perhaps a thousand years as a living community. It may well be, as its people claim, the longest continuously inhabited settlement in America.[6] The Acomas, perched upon their fortress rock, have survived drought, epidemic, famine, war, and oppression not once but several times over. Mind you, the landscape for hundreds of miles around them is littered with the ruins of settlements that did not survive those thousand challenging years, but Acoma did—it sustained itself. The qualities that engendered its astonishing endurance, however, are hardly those that spring to mind in describing most other communities in contemporary America. With Acoma as benchmark, the odds for sustainability would appear stacked against a society that values individualism over community, where consumption is an economic virtue and restraint a vice, and where the phrase *property rights* is a rallying cry and property responsibilities remain undiscussed.

In 1994 I happened to attend a regional hearing of the President's Council on Sustainable Development and had the pleasure of hearing a short speech by Mr. Petuuche Gilbert of Acoma. He explained that having recently been appointed to the Tribal Council, he received instruction from the pueblo elders as to his responsibilities, which included ritual prayers. Taking him to sites in and around the tribe's ancient village, the elders told him he must always "pray first for the world, then for the pueblo, next for his family, and last for himself."

The moral of Mr. Gilbert's story was that as much as resources or development, an enduring community required sustainable values, a telling point. But lest you regard Acoma's approach as excessively pious, please note that much of the praying in the shadow of the mesas these days has more to do with slot machine payoffs than with sustainability. The pueblo's latest development venture, sustainable or not, is Sky City Casino. Its advertising come-ons invite us to "share the heritage."

Acoma is not alone for having contradictions. When we look elsewhere for lessons or expressions of sustainability, we are apt to find equal ambiguity, paradox, and irony. Within the environmental movement, claims of sustainability are made for the most heterogeneous projects: logging regimes, subdivisions with bike trails, ecotourism programs, groundwater management plans, community organizing initiatives, etc. Excluding for the moment those ventures that, whether from shamelessness or ignorance, are mere fund-raising ploys, most sustainable development proposals pursue one or more of three strategies.

The first involves the development of sustainable regimes for harvest of natural resources, such as fish or timber. The record of achievement of the United States in this area is not reassuring. Two of the most forthright legislative expressions of a philosophy of sustainability are the Magnuson Fishery Conservation and Management Act of 1976 and the Multiple Use Sustained Yield Act of 1960. The former guided national policy during the decline and final collapse of New England's saltwater fishery, which it was supposed to have safeguarded, and the latter, together with subsequent legislation that equally espoused the goal of "sustained yield," provided guidance for the liquidation of most of the old growth temperate rain forests in the Pacific Northwest.

Such remarkable failures deserve study and, to a degree, have received it.

Mathematician Donald Ludwig and two colleagues, writing in *Science* in 1993, stated that all the sustainable development programs they studied had ended in failure. Invocations of sustainability notwithstanding, "resources are inevitably overexploited, often to the point of collapse or extinction."

The reasons for this are various, but they center on some common themes:

— Schemes for resource harvest are always geared for maximum "allowable" economic returns.

— The models on which those schemes are based — which determine what is allowable — reflect at best only what is known at the time they are created, which is never all that we need to know.

— Full scientific agreement on the validity of the models or on the data that goes into or comes out of them never exists. Among other things, this means that the judgment of what is allowable is ultimately not a scientific decision but a political and economic one that bears the influence and borrows the legitimacy of "science."[7]

Notwithstanding that the findings of the Ludwig team may be contradicted in some instances by management of local game populations or by certain agricultural regimes, their pragmatic analysis of state-regulated harvest systems constitutes an important cautionary tale (another story!) that is especially applicable where high economic values are at stake.

A second major strategy embraced by sustainable development programs centers on the problem of "getting the numbers right." Here, at least at the outset, both libertarians and central planners find agreement on sustainability's desired end, if not the means to achieve it. The core idea behind this strategy is that the prices at which goods trade should include the costs of the environmental impacts that attend them; that is, markets should "internalize environmental costs"[8] rather than, in an economic sense, debiting these costs against the environmental commons, an "asset" that otherwise declines in productivity and habitability with each corruptive debit. If the true costs of air and water pollution, resource depletion, health effects, and so forth attach to the prices of the goods and services responsible for them, the market would reward "clean" undertakings and induce the steady formation of capital to mitigate the effects of unavoidable depletion. The emphasis here is on *development*, which is assumed to be sustainable provided its externalities are responsibly accounted and paid for.

Not surprisingly this approach has won at least the nominal support of industrial nations with growth-oriented economies.[9] It is far less popular, however, in developing countries, where a third main strategy takes precedence. Writing recently in the journal *Environment,* Tanvi Nagpal reports that Third World advocates of sustainable development take a different but by no means uniform tack. Based on contacts with individuals in thirty-four countries, Nagpal concludes that while "sustainable development is a buzzword in even the smallest African countries, and commissions are being formed around the world to devise national and regional plans . . . there is no prototypical African or Asian definition of a sustainable future."[10] Still, there are common themes. Nagpal asserts that most Third World conceptions of sustainable development postulate thorough-going political and social reform, together with protection for indigenous and traditional cultures, as a precondition for a sustainable future. Most of these conceptions further contemplate a sweeping redistribution of wealth and of economic power.[11]

Obviously the differences among different visions — or stories — of sustainable development reflect the needs and biases of the people who generate them. People in industrial countries frequently emphasize sustaining development. People in developing nations emphasize the need to develop sustainable (read: more equitable) social systems.[12]

But the differences between the stories may be narrowing. Among scholars and, especially, philanthropists (whose grants sustain most experiments in this area), the principal terms of discussion seem to be shifting from *sustainable development* to *sustainable communities* or *sustainability,* expressed, it would seem, as generally and ambiguously as possible.[13] If all this seems vague and hard to pin down — rather like nailing Jell-O to a wall — rest assured that it seems that way also to many of the people involved in "sustainability" projects. Says one, "In this field, umbrella terms, which foster inclusivity, also substitute for specifics. . . . The field needs greater intellectual clarity, more rigor in its analysis of what works and how to achieve success, and a clear sense of the questions and challenges facing it."[14]

It will be interesting, however, to see if such clarity can be forthcoming, for any calculation of sustainability necessarily involves a large number of interdependent variables, and deciding which ones to include, let alone fixing their values, is a task of daunting complexity. As though to acknowledge this, one of the more sophisticated experiments in "sustainability" (at least rhetorically) borrows heavily from complexity theory and conceives of south Florida as a "complex adaptive system" bearing resemblance to other complex adaptive systems of far different scale and character (e.g., immune systems, economies, ecosystems). This enterprise, the so-called Sustainable Everglades Initiative, defines itself not in terms of specific goals but as a process intended to *capture and utilize new learning.* Its purpose is not to achieve a desired state but to accumulate a capacity for resilience and flexibility. Without distinguishing between ecosystems and social or cultural systems, its advocates assert that the goal of the initiative is to build "the adaptive capacity of the entire south Florida system."[15]

This approach encourages participants to accept uncertainty as an unavoidable condition of their undertaking and to see their efforts as experiments in adaptation. In theory, the only constants in such an effort are the values that motivate it. These values, variously expressed, seem to give equal emphasis to the improvement of environmental and social conditions.

The gradual drift of the story of sustainability away from pure economics and toward a more inclusive, if ambiguous and uncertain, embrace of social and political change, has now reached high levels of officialdom. In the United States the 1996 report of the aforementioned President's Council on Sustainable Development identifies political reform as integral even to the task of "getting the numbers right." It specifically recommends increased involvement of local communities in natural resource decisions, with federal authorities playing a facilitating rather than determinative role.[16]

It is perhaps dangerous to attribute much significance to this or any other such commission, except to observe that here is yet another banner in the political breeze that points in the direction of a devolution of power from the federal center toward states and localities. Interestingly, we seem headed away from the highly centralized Progressive model for resource management and toward an approximation of the political relationships recommended in what may have been America's first comprehensive plan for sustainable resource development, at least in the West. The author of the plan was John Wesley Powell, who explained and defended it in extensive testimony before Congress and also published it in his 1878 *Report on the Lands of the Arid Region*, as well as in a series of three articles he published in *Century Magazine* in 1890.[17]

Powell's plan embodied some interesting contradictions, which, incidentally, are also frequently embedded in contemporary rhetoric about sustainable development. Powell believed in local control of natural resources — but only after thorough central planning. He believed in the dispersal of wealth through many small units of property ownership — but only if they might be aggregated, as necessary, to achieve economies of scale and collective economic power. He believed in the moral superiority of an essentially populist agrarian democracy — but also in the vital necessity of advanced scientific knowledge and of the need for centralized institutions, staffed by experts, to dispense it.

In Powell's day the American West was a "developing country" careening forward in the full tilt of westward movement and development. Powell's plan, in which he advocated creation of watershed-based "commonwealths" throughout the arid lands, would have required the arrest of that momentum and a substantial pause in such vital activities as the filing of land entries, development of water resources, and the organization of political subdivisions — all this while the business of planning for the watershed commonwealths was completed. His insistence on deliberation was unrealistic; indeed, it contradicted the prevailing stories of the day, which described the West as a land of opportunity and emphasized the importance of seeking one's fortune, of pursuing happiness. We may ask whose nature was more human — that of the methodical and relentlessly rational Powell or that of the impatient western senators and their equally impatient constituents, who insisted that no governmental authority should slow their self-interested progress. Ultimately Powell and his plan were defeated, and "rushes" for land and gold and timber and water proceeded, scarcely checked, as they had previous to Powell and as they proceed today in developing nations around the world. Then as now people who "prayed first for the world" were outmatched if not outnumbered by those who prayed first for themselves. *Homo economicus* carried the day.

But he was not the only actor in the drama. Acoma remained Acoma and prayed in its way; someone besides *economicus* must have been there. And the storyteller, *Homo narrans* (to borrow Max Oelschlaeger's phrase), also played his role in dramas large and small. The point of this talk about stories is not to suggest, as some would have it, that since our accounts of ourselves are only stories, they are all equally true or untrue, or equally conditional. On the contrary, it suggests that because the stories we tell ourselves have important consequences, we bear a duty to examine them rather closely, to measure our honesty against our hypocrisy, to judge, borrowing Socrates' phrase, "whether we assent to what we know." Our stories about our relationship to the environment deserve special scrutiny, for they materially affect prospects for the survival of a great many things — cultures, societies, and a myriad of creatures, including ourselves. Hence the importance today of scrutinizing the many stories we weave about "sustainable development," chimera though it may be.

Consciously or not, humankind is gambling that its use of the planet is sustainable, or can be made to be so. The outcome of this bet, the denouement of this increasingly pressing story, preoccupied Malthus in his day. It justifiably preoccupies a much greater number of people in ours. And why not? No story we can tell is more suspenseful, and none more directly touches our collective self-interest. Again a catchphrase from the advertising for Acoma's Sky City Casino comes to mind: "It's History in the Making."

NOTES

1. Arthur F. McEvoy, "Toward an Interactive Theory of Nature and Culture: Ecology, Production, and Cognition in the California Fishing Industry," *Environmental Review* 11, no. 4 (winter 1987): 289–305.

2. Much of the activity in libertarian resource economics, at least in the West, originates in association with a trio of small private research institutes: the Gallatin Institute in Missoula, Montana; the Thoreau Institute in Oak Grove, Oregon; and PERC (Political Economy Research Center) in Bozeman, Montana. The newsletters (and increasingly the web pages) of these organizations provide quick access to the kinds of thinking they support. One of the better books produced in this quarter is Randall O'Toole, *Reforming the Forest Service* (Covelo, Calif.: Island Press, 1988). O'Toole is the main force behind the Thoreau Institute.

3. Contemporary libertarianism owes much to both social Darwinism and laissez-faire capitalism. The latter-day Spencerians who advocate it place great faith in the efficient self-organization of free markets, notwithstanding that in places like northern New Mexico, Adam Smith's Invisible Hand has proved more than once to be all thumbs. (See, for instance, William deBuys, *Enchantment and Exploitation* [Albuquerque: UNM Press, 1985], 269 ff.)

4. *New York Times,* 7 August 1994, Business section, p. 12.

5. World Commission on Environment and Development, *Our Common Future* (New York: Oxford University Press, 1987), 8.

6. For a history of the pueblo see Ward Alan Minge, *Acoma: Pueblo in the Sky* (Albuquerque: University of New Mexico, 1976, 1991), or Velma Garcia-Mason, "Acoma," in *Southwest,* vol. 9 of *Handbook of North American Indians,* ed. Alfonso Ortiz (Washington, D.C.: Smithsonian, 1979).

7. Donald Ludwig, Ray Hilborn, and Carl Waters, *Science* 260 (April 2, 1993): 17, 36.

8. J. H. Faulkner, "Capital Formation and Sustainable Development," *Business and the Contemporary World,* 6, no. 2 (1994): 69, as quoted by Tanvi Nagpal, "Voices from the Developing World: Progress Toward Sustainable Development," *Environment* 37, no. 8 (1995): 34.

9. This support is embodied in resolutions adopted in 1994 by the United Nations Commission on Sustainable Development. See Nagpal, p. 35.

10. Nagpal, 13, 15.

11. For a full account of Nagpal's study, which is titled "The 2050 Project," see T. Nagpal and C. Foltz, eds., *Choosing Our Future: Visions of a Sustainable World* (Washington: World Resources Institute, 1995).

12. It is worth noting that in either case, the task of "getting the numbers right" or "getting the politics right" precedes the challenge of "getting the ecological relationships right."

13. See, for instance, Stephen Viederman, "Knowledge for Sustainable Development: What Do We Need to Know?" in *A Sustainable World: Defining and Measuring Sustainable Development* (Sacramento, Calif.: International Center for the Environment and Public Policy for IUCN—The World Conservation Union, 1995).

14. Janet Maughan, "Sustainable Communities" (report to the Johnson Foundation, November 1995); ms in author's possession.

15. "Proposal for the Sustainable Everglades Initiative" (paper presented to The Conservation Fund to the John D. and Catherine T. MacArthur Foundation, October 1995); ms in author's possession.

16. President's Council on Sustainable Development, David T. Buzzelli and Jonathan Lash, cochairs, *Sustainable America* (Washington: U.S. Government Printing Office, 1996). Since issuing its master report in February 1996, the council has produced five supplementary reports: *Sustainable Agriculture, Population and Communities, Energy and Transportation, Eco-Efficiency,* and *Sustainable Communities.*

17. John Wesley Powell, *Report on the Lands of the Arid Region of the United States with a More Detailed Account of the Lands of Utah,* H.R. Exec. Doc. 73, 45th Cong. 2d sess., 1878 (the report was republished, edited by Wallace Stegner, by Harvard University Press in 1962); and J. W. Powell, "The Irrigable Lands of the Arid Region," "The Non-Irrigable Lands of the Arid Region," and "Institutions for the Arid Lands," *Century Magazine* (March, April, and May 1890).

CHAPTER SIX

WE WERE BORN TO IT

Native Americans, Fire, and
Environmental Cultural Continuity

John Herron

I n the July 1930 issue of *American Forests and Forest Life,* Joseph
Halm, a firefighter on the Coeur d'Alene National Forest, recounted
his experiences in the great fire year of 1910.

"For weeks forest rangers with crews of men had been fighting in a vain
endeavor to hold in check the numerous fires which threatened the very
heart of the great white-pine belt.... For days an ominous, stifling pall of
smoke had hung over the valleys and mountains. Crews of men, silent and
grim, worked along the encircling fire trenches. Bear, deer, elk, and mountain lions stalked glazed-eyed and restless through the camps, their fear of
man overcome by a greater terror. Birds, bewildered, hopped about in the
thickets, their song subdued, choked by the stifling smoke and oppressive
heat.... The fragrance of summer flowers had given way to the tang of dead
smoke. Withered ferns and grasses were covered by a hoar-frost of gray
ashes. Men, red-eyed and sore of lung, panted for a breath of untainted
air.... All nature seemed tense, unnatural, and ominous.... [Suddenly] as if
by magic, sparks were fanned to flames which licked the trees into one great
conflagration.... A great wall of fire was coming out of the Northwest. The
wind had risen to hurricane velocity. . . . banners of incandescent flames
[reached toward] the sky. The hissing, roaring flames, the terrific crashing
and rending of falling timber was deafening, terrifying. . . . charred twigs
came sifting out of the ever-darkening sky. The resinous smoke had become
darker, the air even more oppressive and quiet. A few yards below [our

position] the [forest] became a roaring furnace, a threatening hell. If the wind changed, a single blast from this inferno would wipe us out. . . . Out of the underbrush dashed our foreman, arriving still carrying his ax, 'She's jumped a mile across the canyon,'.he said. . . . 'Looks bad.'"[1]

This story, written with all the flair of a Hollywood script, goes on at length — more heat, more flame, more drama — and as you might expect, these men performing "superhuman feats" win in the end. But as this narrative unfolds, the story takes on added significance. This battle with fire becomes "a fight with . . . an evil beast" where men struggle to preserve the natural order. Fire becomes the rhetorical strategy to frame the relationship between humans, nature, and human nature. In the human effort to contain out-of-control nature, wildfire is the foil to set off moral behavior from immoral action.

This use of fire as a window into understanding human behavior marks other forms of nature writing as well. Arthur Carhart, a well-known conservationist, author, and the subject of another essay in this volume, had a less well-known alter ego, that of writing mass-produced pulp fiction nature stories. But like his more mainstream environmental writing, his fiction tried to establish through prose an understanding of the proper relation between humans and nature. One of these stories, *Through the Red Dusk,* written in 1926, is one of my favorites. Set in a battle over grazing rights, the large stockholder, supported by the friendly Forest Ranger, fight the land-grabbing homesteaders and the fires these "dry-landers" started to destroy both the stockman's cattle and Forest Service land. In describing the scene his heroes faced, Carhart narrates, "Whipped by a wind sucking up the cañon . . . the red fiend of the forest had [raced] over the grass and was sucking in the life of young trees. Grass dead as hay whiffed up like powder. . . . Smoke clouded the valley . . . as the night wind shot fire into the air. Dry weather, thick, dry lodgepole pine, and wind, doomed the valley. Lurid twilight now filled the valley as the fire leaped and the smoke curtain was swayed by the wind. It was a ghastly light — the dawn-light of an inferno. Time and again hot stinging smoke [pierced] their lungs, but they fought on, through the red dusk."[2] Once again, as you might imagine, our ranger hero emerges successful from this battle with nature and, adding a nice touch, also gets the girl. Carhart, like Halm, uses fire and the effort to control it to illuminate the role the environment should play in a human-created and -dominated order. Reflecting the commonly held view of the first half of the twentieth century, Carhart saw fire as both unnatural and destructive. Perhaps more significant to Carhart, however, this "red fiend of the forest" was started by individuals who were not in tune with environmental ways, men who represented a destructive ethos. Following human inclination to interpret natural events as social lessons, nature as fire develops into the avenging angel of natural mismanagement. Fire creates a natural value system, or rather creates values *in* nature that become barometers of human behavior. Simply stated, good people put fires out, bad people let them burn. Standing as the counter to pristine nature, fire becomes an indictment of the ignorant human behavior that led to its rise. From this perspective, these fire tales are now able to tell us as much about society and human nature as about nature and the environment. Fires have burned across our earth for thousands of years, but the fires that most capture our attention are the ones that involve human action, human heroes, and human villains.

As these accounts illustrate, few other natural phenomena lace our language with such powerful significance as does fire. Etymologists tell us that words for fire are among the oldest in many languages and that pictographical representations of fire often predate symbols for humans themselves.[3] While it is clear that humans controlled fire before they could create it, the human acquisition of fire remains the subject of scientific controversy. Working with traces of burned bones in South Africa, anthropologist Raymond Dart advanced the theory that the primates between apes and humans — *Australopithecus prometheus* — kept fire in their caves.[4] Other scientists advanced different theories, but regardless of opinion about the moment of human acquisition of fire, the placement of fire within human societies remains a key element in the emergence of human culture and civilization.

Once elevated to a significant position in civilization, the influence of fire spread. The symbolism associated with the language of fire, for example, runs the spectrum from the moral equivalent of war, pitting man against nature, to representations of nature's effort to balance itself, to baptism and rebirth, even to the illumination of the fundamental questions of life and death.[5] And yet this metaphysical understanding of nature's most destructive "disturbance" has pulled fire out of the realm of the natural. When humans insist on viewing fire in human terms, fire is interpreted as ahistorical and often drawn out of its needed context. Returning to Halm's recollection, *"All nature seemed tense, unnatural and ominous."* Apparently Halm hadn't been keeping up with his humanities scholarship, because two decades of anthropology, literary criticism, and history illustrate that nature is never as natural as it seems. Molded, shaped, used, guided, preserved, recorded, and importantly, understood by humans, nature is at base a human construction. A principle element of this belief is that all of society — how we live, how we choose to interact with one another, and, significantly, our perceptions of ourselves and of nature itself — are part of a historical context given meaning only through the cultures that consume them. Our attitudes toward nature are clearly affected by the constraints of our own setting, and these ideas of the natural world never exist outside a cultural context. In short, there is no universal nature of nature.[6]

All too often, however, efforts to explain natural diversity rely on transhistorical definitions that gloss over the complexity that frames the relationship between humans and nature. As these writings on fire demonstrate, the "natural" and the "human" are often assigned universal characteristics that reduce the intimate connection between these two worlds into little more than natural parables, human efforts to make sense of their world. But nature matters to human culture, and any exploration of nature requires an understanding of the intricate web that shapes human-nature interaction.

Our approach to fire should be no different, for fire remains a multiple phenomenon. On one very base level, fire is a chemical process where a series of reactions between oxygen and fuel creates combustion and the production of heat that results in decomposition and oxidation. Fire is also a natural biological event. Natural systems are more than collections of chemical components, and fire remains an integral element in the maintenance of natural biotas and ecosystems. These processes are so endemic to our landscape that rarely does even a microregion on earth escape the effects of wildfire. While most of us remain intimately familiar with the annual summer fires that rage across the American West, equally significant is the burning of the Chinese forest, the hills of New Zealand, and the African plain. Many of these ecosystems adapt themselves to fire so well that they not only accept wildfire but, as the lodgepole pine and black spruce illustrate, require its force of renewal for community survival. Many animals also, from the pine warbler to the North American brown bear, not only evolved to survive fire but depend on postfire regrowth for habitat needs. Perhaps more profound than chemical reactions and environmental symbiosis is the fact that fire, possessing unique qualities that make it both social and ecological, is also a powerful element of culture.[7] Not just a process or an event, fire is also an artifact, a thing. Just as fire behavior is affected by the geographical setting in which it burns, fire is also affected by the cultural setting within which it occurs. A freshly struck Ohio bluetip and a nuclear explosion are found on the extremes of the same fire continuum, but each holds vastly different cultural significance. Environmental historian Stephen Pyne stated that as part of a fire civilization, "We are uniquely fire creatures [living] on a uniquely fire planet." Understanding this connection helps us to realize the context of the very language that defines this relationship.

Social scientists long recognized the influence of the natural world on human affairs, but until recently few adequately explored the complex dialogue that informs these connections between human society and the natural environment. As this anthology tries to demonstrate, part of the explanation lies in historical assumptions about human nature and human culture. The concept of human nature has a long and varied history, but so too does the idea of human culture. Like other symbols, culture often means whatever we use it to mean, but an environmental understanding of culture and one with a particular significance to this essay comes from historian and author William deBuys. "Culture," writes deBuys, "provides a filter through which people perceive the environment around them and their relation to it. It screens out certain influences or possibilities while allowing others to pass on to awareness."[8] The diffusion of influences through our cultural filters remains important because regardless of definition, part of the problem with the analysis of the interaction between humans, culture, and their environment is one of perspective. Often exclusionary, efforts to understand the full implications of human presence on the land overlook many who actively shaped their environment. In this effort to explore the linkages between culture and the environment, historians only recently discovered what anthropologists and ethnographers have known for decades—that this process of cultural representation is inescapably contingent, historical, and contestable.[9]

The lingering problems that affect cultural interrogation are still evident in the historical analysis of Native Americans. Our interpretation of Native American human nature contains a substantial degree of enthnocentrism; as in relations with the natural world, two visions of Indian human nature dominate. One view holds that Native Americans are the "perfect embodiment of the positive qualities of nature; Edenic innocence, primitive simplicity, generosity . . . and self-transcendence."[10] Philosopher Joseph Epes Brown claims, "All American Indian peoples possessed . . . a metaphysic of nature . . . a manifest reverence for the naturalized world."[11] In a similar fashion, J. Donald Hughes in *American Indian Ecology* writes of America as an "unspoiled continent" before white arrival and that everywhere Indians "lived in careful balance" with Mother Earth.[12] Calvin Martin wrote in his controversial 1978 *Keepers of the Game*, "There were certain elements of [Indian] ideologies all seemed to share, the most outstanding being a genuine respect for the welfare of other life forms."[13] The problems with such an approach are many. Most significantly, the assertion that Native Americans lived in a pristine state of nature ignores the presence of any human hand that shaped and reshaped precontact America. There is little debate that native and nonnative societies often possess different natural cosmologies, but to naturalize native peoples denies them their very history and culture.[14] As Richard White explains, "We are pious toward Indian peoples, but we don't take them seriously; we don't credit them with the capacity to make changes. Whites readily grant certain nonwhites a 'spiritual' or 'traditional' knowledge that is timeless . . . [a non]contingent knowledge in a contingent world."[15]

On the other side of these assumptions of a universal human nature for Native Americans stands the dehumanized Indian. Portrayed as simply another element of the inanimate world — a stone in the path, a tree in the field — native peoples blend into the landscape as the background to all stories other than their own. The misconception is that Native Americans, as an intrinsic element of nature, are inside nature and are therefore incapable of modifying it. Like sculptors' clay, Native Americans and the natural environment are blended together by outside forces but remain unable to shape the world they inhabit. While a generation of historians have produced a number of works concentrating on how Indian peoples did indeed shape the natural world they inhabited, the view that the Native American presence did not alter the landscape still receives a surprising amount of ink.[16] Constructing their narratives to place their causes on center stage, environmental writers often manipulate the drama inherent in their stories. As part of his 1992 history of the environmental movement, *A Fierce Green Fire,* writer Philip Shabecoff traced the westward journey of Lewis and Clark. The "awestruck" expedition, writes Shabecoff, "came to the . . . Rocky Mountains and then to the Coast ranges" and found those areas "unchanged by humans." Shabecoff continues, "Save for the changes in the Indians' way of life brought about by the guns, horses, metals, and other European imports, which may have had some impact on the environment, the plains remained as they had been in pre-Columbian days."[17] His definitions of "unchanged" and "impact" must differ substantially from my own. Following this line of reasoning, in *The End of Nature,* writer William McKibben states, "It is hard for us to credit that only a hundred and twenty years ago the valley of the Colorado-the Grand Canyon-was a blank spot on the maps of the Southwest."[18] In this case, the "blank spot" was inhabited for centuries by numerous native groups. This pattern holds for many other travel accounts of men like Kit Carson, Daniel Boone, Zebulon Pike, and even environmental heroes like John Muir and John Wesley Powell. While interesting characters to be sure, the tendency of contemporary environmental advocates to posit that these white explorers journeyed into a virgin world is absurd. Unlike Neil Armstrong, these white travelers did not encounter nature in the raw but rather nature remade, a landscape already shaped by Native Americans. Of course, Indian efforts to influence their environment varied profoundly by region. Various agriculture methods, hunting styles, and living arrangements each left localized marks on the land, yet despite these differences in nearly every landscape the clearest transformation of nature was done with fire.

In its most controlled form, fire was used for cooking. By affecting the division of social space, fire changed eating habits by making meats more digestible, many plants now edible, and preservation of perishable foodstuffs a possibility.[19] Other obvious domestic uses of fire include a much needed source of light and heat. The construction and placement of hearths influenced native building techniques, family social dynamics, and even community relations. Fire not only shaped domestic space but natural space as well. Narrow trails through the tangled forest hindered movement and provided dangerous concealment to hunting targets and potential enemies. Fire removed this brush and undergrowth, improving visibility, travel, and hunting. This periodic burning of the landscape also removed weeds and fostered plant growth, including berries, beans, nuts, and natural grains. Herding Indians on the Great Plains regularly burned the prairie to stimulate grass growth for horse fodder.[20] In his journals, George Catlin describes this process of annual Indian burns, which "were voluntarily done for the purpose of getting a fresh crop of grass, for the grazing of their horses, and also for easier traveling during the next summer, when there will be no old grass to lie upon the prairies, entangling the feet of man and horse."[21] Fire was also an important step in returning nutrients to the soil, in maintaining agricultural fertility, and in creating savannalike habitats that would encourage fauna growth.[22] After harvest, fire cleared fields of vermin and disease. Broadcast wildfires warded off predators and drove away pests, including mosquitoes, flies, and moths. Fire became an important weapon in warfare. Fire could flush out enemies, harass army troops, cover movements with smoke, or be employed as part of a scorched-earth campaign.[23] For many native societies, fire also possessed a sacred character and was an integral element in religious ceremonies and purification rituals. Beyond its role in ceremony, fire was linked to entertainment. Fire was used in games, mock battles, and celebrations. Lewis and Clark both noted in their journals the torching of fir trees as part of a nighttime spectacle.[24] Probably most significantly, fire was used for hunting. Smoke and fire "flushed bees from their hives, raccoons out of their dens, and bears out of their caves." At night, torches spotlighted game and drew fish to canoes to be speared. Fire aided in the hunt for deer in the Northeast, alligators in Florida, rabbits in the Southwest, antelope in the Great Basin, buffalo in the plains, and moose in Alaska.[25] Despite this wide range of uses, this remains only a sampling of the Indian appropriation of fire. In exploring the significance of fire to Native Americans, it is hard to overstate the effect of fire on native culture and the

American landscape. Part of the noble savage myth assumes "that past societies—in touch with nature as they had to be—were also in harmony with it. They may not have dominated nature in the way that we hope to, but by being subordinate to it, they may perhaps have lived sustainably with it."[26] Changing the land, however, like native uses of fire, also marks a change in power. Native Americans are not symbolic Indians living in natural harmony with the environment but complex thinking human beings who actively construct the world around them.

From the earliest moments that Europeans explored the American Southwest or stepped ashore in New England, the many dimensions associated with these Indian fire practices were well known. Throughout American history, Native American fire techniques influenced conceptions of land use, management, and environmental interaction. But as American society began to fill in the continent, Indian fire was not without conflict or controversy. While many became captivated by the nature of Indian fire, it was the uncontrolled fire of native peoples that finally captured the attention of white society.[27] In 1878 John Wesley Powell, director of the United States Geographical and Geological Survey of the Rocky Mountain Region, wrote *Report on the Lands of the Arid Region of the United States*. In this report, which Powell hoped to use as a plan for western development, he wrote that fires "annually destroy large districts of timber . . . and [that] this destruction is on a scale so vast that the amount taken from the lands for industrial purposes sinks by comparison into insignificance." Powell noted the importance of timber resources to American development and stated that the "protection of the entire Arid Region of the United States is reduced to one single problem—can these forests be saved from fire?" Powell believed that if protected timber growth in the West could eventually fulfill all "the industrial interests . . . the country will require." While the "conditions under which these fires rage" Powell concluded were primarily climatic—"lack of adequate humidity and rainfall"—the main causation for these fires was Indians and their "wanton desire . . . to destroy that which is of value to the white man." The fires could be greatly curtailed and the American forest "saved" only "by the removal of the Indians."[28]

Beyond these ecological arguments, the debate over Indian fire had other social components as well. From being a nonfactor to being the factor, Native American fire and Native Americans' role in fire management has continually been misunderstood and misrepresented. Before it was believed that fire harmed the environment, early frontier residents recognized Indian burning and wrote of it often in personal diaries and travelers' accounts. When scientific forestry came to the United States in the last decades of the nineteenth century, the application of fire was not considered proper management and, interestingly, Indians were then thought not to burn. In contemporary America, when prescribed fire is again accepted as a key part of any natural regime, it was rediscovered that Indians did burn.[29] The persistent desire to keep Indians natural and to reduce the understanding of Native American human nature to basic primitivism overwhelmed the practical history of the intersections between Native Americans and the natural environment.

Just what was the "natural way" has been open to constant reinterpretation. Assumptions of human nature are historically articulated, and Native American culture was often determined by what contemporary white society thought it should be. Even Powell himself modified his earlier *Arid Land* position as in the last decade of the nineteenth century he began to report the virtues of Indian burning and the favorable influence that fire had on forest cover, water flow, and climate. Powell still maintained that "fire is the enemy of the forest" but argued that "before the white man came the natives systematically burned over the forest lands," protecting the health of the forest ecosystem. Without the controlling efforts of native fire, Powell concluded, "Forests are rapidly disappearing."[30] As the evolving position of Powell demonstrates, Indian fire has always been a hotly contested issue filled with incendiary language sparking numerous debates about proper notions of ecological balance. But what is oddly overlooked in nearly every analysis of Indian fire are issues of environmental management. In yet another incomplete vision of the totality of human efforts to manage their own landscape, Native Americans simply become equated with the fire itself; they are not seen as actively participating in land management or fire control as they begin to blend in with the natural order. Seen as one-dimensional, Indian fire practices are often interpreted without any greater cultural context. "It is one thing if Americans, operating out of European tradition, choose to declare themselves unnatural. . . . it is another to extend that declaration to America's indigenous peoples" and state that Indian burning and fire suppression were not a part of an effort to effect changes on the land.[31] Native Americans were intimately familiar with precepts of resource control and, importantly, fire prevention. Human geographer Carl Sauer mistakenly remarked that the use of fire was a feature of primitive society, fire management of civilized society. "It is my opinion," writes Sauer, "that native peoples have rarely been careful to extinguish their campfires . . . because it did not occur to them to protect the vegetation from fire."[32] While scattered references to careless Indian fire habits appear in the literature, most Native Americans lived in fire environments they helped to create; ignorance of fire control practices had dangerous consequences. One reason behind the failure of larger society to recognize Indian fire suppression efforts is linked to cultural stereotypes. Supported by a naturalist's fallacy that is both anthropocentric and racist, the tangible circumstances of the Native American hand on the land are continually underestimated. Assigning new characteristics to Native American personality traits, Hu Maxwell wrote in 1910, "The Indian is by nature an incendiary" and forest burning is the "Indians' besetting sin." So much of Indian burning is seen as superstition that any effort on the part of natives to manage fire, however systematic, was not seen as scientific but as ritual.[33] Native Americans did environmental modifications, especially with fire, but in "our eurocentric guilt we tend to associate [these changes] only with industrial societies."[34]

Examples of Indian fire prevention and suppression, however, abound in western literature. When Washington Irving went on his tour of the prairies, he wrote of a cooking fire that escaped its rock hearth and threatened the camp. Panic gripped Irving and his companions as "all was hurry-scurry and uproar" when "no one . . . knew how to quell [the fire]." Fortunately for Irving, an Indian guide "and his comrades attacked [the fire] in the Indian mode, beating down the fire with blankets and horse-cloths," and "happily" rescued the camp.[35] Fire suppression is also a theme in western painting and literature. During his career, western artist Charlie Russell painted scenes that depicted a number of different Indian burning practices. Other well-known western painters like Alfred Jacob Miller, A. F. Tait, Frederic Remington, and George Catlin often incorporated native uses of fire into their work. Writers James Fenimore Cooper and Edgar Rice Burroughs also used native fire practices in their stories and essays.[36] Recognition of Indian fire management is only half the story, however, because these examples of Native American fire suppression illustrate that even today, native efforts to manage and extinguish fire remain an important tool to shape the natural environment. The necessities of life in an industrialized system have, obviously, curtailed the extent of Indian burning, but in fire suppression many Indian peoples continue to use fire to alter their environment.

The work of fire suppression is at best dirty and monotonous and at worst dangerous, even deadly, but it is into this work environment that many Native Americans are particularly drawn. Native American firefighters work in fire suppression for a variety of motivations ranging from economic reward to recalling ancestral behaviors like hunting and warfare. Most intriguing, however, are the claims that Native Americans possess a special affinity for working with fire. While the stories contemporary Native American firefighters tell are filled with much of the same drama as those of Halm or Carhart, the significance of their work with fire remains quite different. Marcus Trujillo of the Carson National Forest says, "The strenuous work of fighting fires fits into the traditional hard work ethic of New Mexican Indians." Carlos Yazzie, a

Navajo working for the Gallup, New Mexico, Bureau of Indian Affairs, believes, "We are adapted to it; we have been doing this work our whole life. It is situated to us; it goes back to our traditions." Cornel Cervantes, a Mescalero Apache, says, "The hard work drives us. . . . We, Native people, have stamina and endurance that allows us to do hard, physical work." Jemez firefighter Daniel Loren developed a more straightforward philosophy: "We were born to it; it's what we do."[37] Each of these Native American firefighters repeatedly emphasized the great pride they took from their work with fire. Each of their comments were sprinkled with references to "working in the Indian way," working "like we have always done," and "doing our sacred duty to protect nature." Taken to their extreme, these views come dangerously close to offering an essentialist view of Native American human nature, that Native Americans are naturally more natural. These positions also imply that by simply removing the white human presence from nature, we could more easily return to a state of pristine or virgin wilderness and native land harmony. But these stories also illuminate the problems of removing all humans from nature. Having complex and independent histories, the reality surrounding the encounter between fire and humans has always been more complicated than it appears.

Following many of the same lines of debate as the current concern over wilderness in both popular and academic arenas, our approach to Indian fire has a built-in paradox. If nature to be wild or natural includes a vision of the human as entirely outside nature, then Indians and fire move into the realm of the sublime where illusion and romance dominate. If we recognize Indians' ability to shape their world with fire, then we need to reconceptualize our definitions of natural and unnatural. In contemporary America, natural definitions follow political fault lines, but as recent scholarship demonstrates, nature is "far more dynamic, far more changeable, and far more entangled with human history than popular beliefs about 'the balance of nature' have typically acknowledged."[38] Many of these popular ideas about the environment are based on the notion that if we could just limit human presence, the undisturbed community of nature could endure indefinitely. Removing human ingredients from the recipe, however, does not make nature pure. To return briefly to the debate over wilderness, the one associated problem that plagues the Forest Service and its fire management policies focuses on this ultimate symbol of nature. If one believes wilderness to be a completely natural environment, it would stand to reason that fire as a completely natural process would be a fundamental element or at least a perfect complement to the wilderness ecosystem. Leading down the path toward restoration, wilderness fire management was designed to establish balance and equilibrium by removing the visible forces of human influence so the invisible forces of nature could take over. This newly created landscape does not replicate any scene from nature but rather creates a new nature that in all likelihood never existed. Restoration in nature is always difficult, because where does the process begin and end? My family is currently restoring their ninety-year-old home. One problem they are facing is an eighty-year-old attached porch. To achieve a perfect restoration, does the porch stay or go? In this effort to balance nature, where do Native Americans stay and where do they go? As the intersection between fire and Indian efforts to shape their landscape illustrates, these issues are far more complex. While a vision of natural harmony once dominated, the intricacy of our modern interaction with nature demands a better understanding of this relationship. Fire is not just a natural event occurring in a natural landscape but a mix of constantly reshaping culture and nature. As cultural artifacts, fire and wilderness are products of the social context that not only created them but also gave them meaning. Introduce Native Americans and you add another layer of complexity to this dynamic because for this view to now hold true, Indian presence must be seen as nondisturbing or as unimportant — either way, individual agency is lost for the sake of natural integrity. The examination of Native American human nature calls into question the tendency to appeal to nonhuman nature as the standard measure to judge human nature and human uses of nature. But for better or worse, these worlds have so meshed with our social values that a complete separation would be impossible.[39] In 1954 Loren Eiseley remarked, "Man is himself a flame" because man, like fire, not only consumes but transforms environment and self.[40] There is little question that fire has assisted humans in their journey across the planet; a fuller realization of who used fire illustrates that the line separating civilization from nature is not as distinct as we once thought.

NOTES

Any scholar who works with the topic of fire owes a large debt to the work of Stephen Pyne, and a quick glance at my notes will prove that his ideas dramatically affect this essay.

1. Joseph Halm, "I'll Never Fight Fire with My Bare Hands Again," in *Recollections of the First Forest Rangers of the Inland Northwest,* ed. Hal K. Rothman (Lawrence: University of Kansas, 1994), 159–61.
2. Arthur H. Carhart, *Through the Red Dusk* (Blue Book Magazine Company, 1926), 23–30.
3. Joseph D. Mitchell, "The American Indian: Fire Ecologist," *American Indian Culture and Research Journal* 2, no. 2 (1977), 26.

4. Raymond Dart, "The Makapansgat Proto-Human *Australopithecus prometheus*," *American Journal of Physical Anthropology* 6 (1948), 259.

5. Examples of each style can be found in any sampling of the literature on fire. See, for example, Norman MacClean's *Young Men and Fire* (Chicago: University of Chicago Press, 1992), and Stephen Pyne's *Fire on the Rim: A Firefighter's Season at the Grand Canyon* (New York: Ballantine Books, 1989).

6. These ideas have received significant attention in recent environmental scholarship. For an excellent overview of these concepts see William Cronon, ed., *Uncommon Ground: Toward Reinventing Nature* (New York: Norton, 1995), 23–56.

7. Stephen J. Pyne, *Fire in America: A Cultural History of Wildland and Rural Fire* (Princeton: Princeton University Press, 1982), 3–5; see also William Cronon, "A Place for Stories: Nature, History, and Narrative," *Journal of American History* 78, no. 4 (March 1992), 1347–76.

8. William deBuys, *Enchantment and Exploitation: The Life and Hard Times of a New Mexico Mountain Range* (Albuquerque: University of New Mexico Press, 1985), 9.

9. See James Clifford and George E. Marcus, eds., *Writing Culture: The Poetics and Politics of Ethnography* (Berkeley: University of California Press, 1986).

10. Richard Slotkin, *The Fatal Environment: The Myth of the Frontier in the Age of Industrialization, 1800–1890* (New York: Atheneum, 1985), 53.

11. Joseph Epes Brown, *The Spiritual Legacy of the American Indian* (New York: Crossroad, 1982), 37.

12. J. Donald Hughes, *American Indian Ecology* (El Paso: Texas Western Press, 1983), 5.

13. Calvin Martin, *Keepers of the Game: Indian-Animal Relationships and the Fur Trade* (Berkeley: University of California Press, 1978), 67.

14. For more information see Richard White and William Cronon, "Ecological Change and Indian-White Relations," in *The Handbook of Native American Indians*, vol. 4 (Washington, D.C.: Smithsonian, 1988), 417.

15. Richard White, "'Are You an Environmentalist or Do You Work for a Living?': Work and Nature," in *Uncommon Ground*, 175. ·

16. See W. R. Swagerty, ed., *Scholars and the Indian Experience* (Bloomington: University of Indiana Press, 1984).

17. Philip Shabecoff, *A Fierce Green Fire: The American Environmental Movement* (New York: Hill & Wang, 1992), 23.

18. William McKibbon, *The End of Nature* (New York: Anchor Books, 1989), 54.

19. Loren C. Eiseley, "Man the Fire-Maker," *Scientific American* 191, no. 3 (1954): 56.

20. Richard White, *Roots of Dependency: Subsistence, Environment, and Social Change among the Choctaws, Pawnees, and Navajos* (Lincoln: University of Nebraska Press, 1983), 185.

21. George Catlin, *Letters and Notes on the Manners, Customs, and Conditions of the North American Indians; Written during Eighty Years' Travel among the Wildest Tribes in North America* (New York: Dover, 1973), 19.

22. Carl Sauer, "Fire as the First Great Force Employed by Man," in *Man's Role in the Changing the Face of the Earth*, ed. William L. Thomas, Jr. (Chicago: University of Chicago Press, 1956), 118–125.

23. Mavis Loscheider, "Use of Fire in Interethnic and Intraethnic Relations on the

Northern Plains." *Western Canadian Journal of Anthropology* 7, no. 4 (1977), 82–96.

24. Pyne, *Fire in America,* 71–72.

25. Ibid., 74.

26. Stephen Yearley, "Environmental Challenges," in *Modernity: An Introduction to Modern Societies,* ed. Stuart Hall, David Held, Don Hubert, and Kenneth Thompson (Oxford: Blackwell Press, 1996), 506.

27. Mircea Eliade, *The Sacred and the Profane: The Nature of Religion* (New York: Harcourt Brace Jovanovich, 1959).

28. John Wesley Powell, *Report on the Lands of the Arid Region of the United States with a More Detailed Account of the Lands of Utah,* ed. Wallace Stegner (Cambridge: Harvard University Press, 1962), 25–28.

29. Pyne, *Fire in America,* 81.

30. John Wesley Powell, "The Non-Irrigable Lands of the Arid Region," *Century Magazine* XXXIX (March 1890), 915–19.

31. Pyne, *World Fire,* 242.

32. Sauer, "Fire as the First Great Force," 118.

33. Hu Maxwell, "The Use and Abuse of the Forests by the Virginia Indians," *William and Mary Quarterly,* vol. 19 (1910), 86. See also Henry T. Lewis, "Traditional Uses of Fire by Indians in Northern Alberta," *Current Anthropology* 19, no. 2. (June 1978), 401–402.

34. Dan Flores, "The West That Was," *High Country News,* 18 August 1997, 6.

35. Washington Irving, *A Tour on the Prairies,* ed. John Francis McDermott (Norman: University of Oklahoma Press, 1956), 128.

36. Pyne, *Fire in America,* 78.

37. Carlos Yazzie, interview by author, Gallup, N.M., 15 October 1995; Cornel Cervantes, interview by author, Albuquerque, N.M., 25 October 1995; Daniel Loren, interview by author, Albuquerque, N.M., 27 October 1995.

38. Cronon, *Uncommon Ground,* 24.

39. Pyne, *World Fire,* 238–55.

40. Eiseley, "Man the Fire-Maker," 56.

CHAPTER SEVEN

DUPES, CONSPIRATORS, TRUTH SEEKERS, AND OTHER BREEDS

*A Typology of the Human
Animal in Environmental
History Narratives*

Paul Hirt

Τ his chapter examines the ways environmental historians construct and *people* their narratives. Two things inspired my reflections here. First, my own efforts to categorize and characterize the significant actors who have influenced the history of the national forests in America. To present a compelling environmental and political history of forest management, I had to distill from a large constellation of actors a key cast of individuals and organizations whose activities plausibly explained historical events and provided conceptual order to the narrative. This was not, by any means, a simple task. While constructing the narrative, I regularly agonized over how and when to generalize a group of actors as opposed to differentiating them. For example, whenever I found myself using the labels "timber industry" or "environmentalists," I squirmed in discomfort as I thought about who I was lumping together and all the gradations within those categories that the general terms obscured. On the other hand, whenever I found myself gleefully immersed in the intricate retelling of a controversy with lots of players and lots of angles, I would inevitably find that the narrative had gone Byzantine and that no one found it as interesting as me. Consequently I would resort to erasing and lumping certain characters and events to make the prose crisper and more accessible. That was my practical lesson in the politics of narrative—a politics that I find as troubling as it is fascinating.

The second inspiration for these reflections is a brilliant essay by Bill

Cronon titled "A Place for Stories: Nature, History, and Narrative," in which he deconstructs and reconstructs the act of storytelling in environmental history. It should be required reading for every historian embarked on a book or dissertation. While Cronon focuses mainly on plot and narrative in that essay, my purpose here is to analyze how historians build a cast of characters for their tales; not so much individual characters—although that's an interesting topic too—but *group* actors. Everyone knows the genre: many authors and teachers have written about or taught about whites, blacks, elites, minorities, Republicans, socialists, feminists, racists. . . . The list is endless. We all employ these categories, yet we all know they are to a certain extent artificial. They can be helpful or they can be profoundly distorting, depending on context. Regardless of how you feel about it, however, some categorizing of human actors is unavoidable for most historical narratives. Here I want to examine a few cases of how environmental historians have peopled their narratives and assigned to them character traits such as motive and understanding. In the process I raise more questions than I answer, but I hope the examination at least sheds some light on the helpful and distorting aspects of this enterprise.

Much environmental history is "problem oriented": What caused the dust bowl? What led to the decline of fisheries in California? How have cities tried to address pollution and waste problems? Why have minorities and the poor suffered more from environmental problems than the affluent majority? My own book, *A Conspiracy of Optimism,* asks: What is at the root of contemporary forest controversies and how might we achieve a more equitable and sustainable relationship with our national forests?

In framing a narrative that illuminates problems, environmental historians almost by necessity must identify some social group or ideology or mode of economic production or psychological characteristic of our species as a key explanation for the problem. Likewise, to point to possible solutions, some human characteristic or mode of production or institution must be cited as preferable to whatever led to the problem. To illuminate a historical problem, then, we must ask and answer the following questions:

Who acts? Or who has the power and agency to shape events?
How and why do they act the way they do, and what results from those actions?
Conversely, among those affected by environmental changes, we might also ask, Who *lacks* the power to influence outcomes and why?

Thus environmental history narratives are still greatly concerned about humans and human nature.

With the possible exception of biographies, identifying actors requires a writer to become a taxonomist of sorts, to lump or split people into more or less coherent groups. For example, do we treat men and women the same or differently when we talk about attitudes toward the environment? Do we distinguish urban from rural people when we discuss resource consumption? When considering who gains and who loses from environmental protection policies, do we break society into the traditional three classes—working class, middle class, and upper class—or do we subdivide that further or create different categories entirely? When discussing environmental justice issues, do we lump together minorities as a group or pull them apart by race and ethnicity? The answers, of course, depend on what you are trying to explain. As Cronon pointed out in his essay, your narrative strategy profoundly shapes the content of your analysis. My point here is that your narrative strategy also drives your choice of human subjects and your characterization of human nature.

As an aside, it is worth noting that this endeavor to lump and split leads to what some scholars refer to as "privileging" some actors and "erasing" others. When we identify the actors in the play, we often write a good chunk of the population out of the script entirely. Every narrative does this to one degree or another. Accounting for those who were invisible in a story can sometimes substantially alter the conclusions; other times not. The most successful problem-oriented histories don't leave out actors who are central to the problem being analyzed. This initial choice of who to illuminate and who to ignore is one of the most important decisions a scholar makes when constructing a narrative.

Once you have lumped and split your actors into more or less coherent units, then you must attribute thought, intention, and action to them, as well as interaction among them. You must give individuals and groups of individuals characteristics, then describe their relations. Once again this is a process of privileging and erasing. For example, Donald Worster's book *Rivers of Empire* offers the following assessment of actors, their characteristics, and their relations in the western water development drama:

Accepting the authority of engineers, scientists, economists, and bureaucrats along with the power of capital, the common people become a herd. . . . Instead of maturing into autonomous, rational individuals capable of deciding ultimate issues, as one side of the Enlightenment promised they would all do in the modern age, they instead become lifelong wards of the corporation and the state. Sensing their own impotence in the midst of so much general power, they may feel anger welling up inside them; but they do not know whom or what to blame, so thoroughly have they absorbed and internalized the ruling ideas, so completely have they lost the capacity for critical thought.[1]

Here in this brief passage we have a taxonomy that includes (1) a monolithic capitalist elite; (2) a technological elite split into engineers, scientists, and economists; and (3) the undifferentiated "common people." The capitalist elite and the managerial/technical elite work together to reconstruct nature in pursuit of wealth and power. The rest of society becomes a passive "herd," dupes following the person in front of them to who knows what destination, "wards of the state" sedated by the comfort and security offered by the architects of the hydraulic society. The masses in this vision lack both freedom and understanding, which the managerial and capitalist elite presumably enjoy a larger measure of—although the elite's understanding has a dark side: it is wedded to an ethos of maximum control over nature for maximum wealth, an ideology that Worster warns will ultimately destroy both nature and liberty. The passage is powerful, compelling, and instructive, but it also erases a great deal, and it is within those blank areas, within those lumped categories, that different historians with different interests and different conceptions of the environmental problem find a different sort of taxonomy.

I use this passage from Worster because he is one of the profession's most accomplished narrators, and the passage provides an excellent starting point for a discussion of how environmental historians characterize human nature in their tales. For the remainder of this presentation I will examine three narratives from my own field of forest history, delineating the actors that emerge from those histories, the human characteristics they exhibit, the narrative strategies that give rise to those human types, and some of the limitations and opportunities associated with each narrative's cast of characters. I believe this kind of analysis can be fruitfully applied across the spectrum of environmental history—indeed, into all historical fields.

Forest histories have been around for decades and come in many genres, from popular, journalistic accounts to comprehensive academic tomes, from organizational histories of agencies that manage forests to studies of ecological change and human responses. In each case, the authors select a piece of the forest history puzzle and pursue a particular story line within that framework. The specific subject matter, the story line, and the narrative strategy all coalesce to determine who appears as actors in the tale and how they are portrayed.

Some stories are fairly simple, with limited and basically one-dimensional actors. An example is Ashley L. Schiff's *Fire and Water: Scientific Heresy in the Forest Service*.[2] Schiff's book is a classic analysis of bureaucratic behavior. It focuses on how the Forest Service has managed fire and water in the national forests. The story line is one of crusading administrators perverting science in pursuit of policy agendas. The only actors in the book are administrators, scientists, private landowners, and a generalized "public." Most everyone else is invisible, as is the diversity within these broad categories of actors. Schiff's strategy is to convince readers that scientists said one thing about the influence of fire on forests and the influence of forests on streams while administrators clung to an alternative and erroneous view wedded to a policy agenda. Furthermore, Schiff wants to show that policies based on unproved theories about fire and water caused environmental problems and economic inefficiencies, and those problems could be solved by rigidly segregating science from politics.

According to Schiff, the fire issue boiled down to this: In the early years of this century, the Forest Service adopted a campaign to totally exclude fire from all timberlands, even though some forests seemed to have coevolved with frequent fires and some fires clearly had desirable consequences.[3] Basing its campaign primarily on a fear of uncontrolled conflagrations, the agency decided all fires in all commercial forests should be suppressed. Anyone offering the view that some fires actually served a beneficial purpose was ignored, refuted, or ridiculed.

In support of fire suppression Schiff claims the Forest Service developed carrot-and-stick incentives for landowners to conform to its anti-wildfire policies. Then, he says, agency administrators intentionally generated conflicting data on the effects of fire in order to weaken the arguments of opponents of the policy. This paints administrators as unethical, Machiavellian manipulators in contrast to the scientists who approached the world honestly, armed only with their data.

The general public appears briefly as an external force to be reckoned with, though it seems to have little autonomous agency. Schiff claims that when the agency promoted fire suppression as a "public" campaign, a pro-suppression momentum developed among the masses. Here is how Schiff characterizes the general public as an actor in his narrative: "Evangelism and the appeal to 'mob psychology' won converts to 'the cause.' In so doing, it created a commitment to promulgated doctrine, and this inevitably impaired the ability of the Service to retract statements later demonstrated by research to be inaccurate."[4] Thus the general public shows up as a "mob" converting unthinkingly to the administrator/evangelist's sermons on the evils of fire. Schiff's take on the nature of the masses as a "mob" is not too different from Worster's take on the masses as a "herd." This characterization is fairly common in environmental history and serves to heighten narrative tension. If the bulk of the human population unthinkingly moves in a dangerous direction, then changing course becomes exceedingly important *and* exceedingly difficult. It is the lemming metaphor and the freight train metaphor rolled into one. Drama results. This situation also creates a heroic role for the person who reveals the danger and points to a safe course — a role that, not surprisingly, usually embodies the narrator.

Schiff's view of human nature in this study assumes not only that scientists are naturally objective but that administrators are naturally manipulative and lack a commitment to the truth. He also assumes the primary source of compromising pressures on agency scientists comes from the administrative arm of the agency. This ignores a whole spectrum of influences on scientists, including personal biases, professional biases, occupational allegiances, political pressures external to the agency, and budgetary constraints. At least as common as incidents in which good science is ignored or suppressed by an administrator are incidents in which researchers tailor their studies to fit their own interests or policy commitments.

Moreover, administrators and scientists are quite often the same person — which poses a special problem for Schiff, who portrays them as clearly distinct. All the chiefs of the Forest Service, for example, have been trained foresters. Some, in fact, rose to the head of the agency through its research branch. When does such a person cease being an objective scientist and become instead a manipulative administrator? Schiff never acknowledges this ambiguity.

One-dimensional assessments of human nature like Schiff's make for passable organizational theory but are very unhelpful in explaining history. Every scientist and administrator in Schiff's story, in fact, was a complex individual holding sometimes contradictory values and commitments. Moreover, the agency itself is fragmented by professions and allegiances and authorities. Plus the whole policy implementation environment is fragmented into competing and overlapping systems and subsystems. These complexities must be acknowledged to build a plausible history of fire and water management on the national forests. We must be cautious, however, when decrying simple narratives. Overly complex characterizations of actors and their natures can so convolute a narrative that readers lose track and the explanation is lost. The demands of audiences and the constraints of the narrative form require a certain level of generalization. Finessing a balance is the challenge.

A good contrast to Schiff's viewpoint is Alston Chase's recent book *In a Dark Wood*.[5] Chase is an Ivy League–trained philosopher turned environmental journalist writing about the forest controversy in the Northwest. Interested in more than the Forest Service, he has a much richer cast of human characters than Schiff, but they are just as one-dimensional.

His book's subtitle, "The Fight Over Forests and the Rising Tyranny of Ecology," indicates his central thesis: that in the battle over the allocation of northwest forest resources a cabal of federal bureaucrats, environmental activists, and ecosystem ecologists have usurped political power in pursuit of their preservationist agenda, instituting a regulatory tyranny backed by a false and dangerous ecological ideology masquerading as science. This errant path away from liberal humanism and toward biocentrism in the last few decades threatens to lead to both social and environmental disaster, he argues. The dramatic tension in Chase's narrative revolves around this "war between good and evil" rhetoric and his efforts to illuminate a safe path for society around the land mines of bad science, irrational environmentalism, antihumanist radicalism, and inept, antilibertarian government. Chase tries to explain where we lost our way and how we can get "back on track."

The cast in this play is fairly extensive (421 pages of text!), but Chase lumps the actors into groups that represent different positions in his moral drama. More interested in humans than in organizations and more interested in ideas than material relations, Chase's taxonomy largely hinges on what a person believes. As a former philosopher, Chase is convinced that ideas are the measure of life and the driving force of history. Thus the villain in his story, he claims in his preface, is not a person but an idea — "an idea that society had embraced but did not understand."[6] The dangerous idea is "biocentrism," which actually turns out to comprise a couple of pop ecology ideas: that there is a "balance of nature" that must be maintained and that the ecosystem as a whole has an integrity that is more important than its individual parts. These "false" ideas, adopted by the uncomprehending masses, have led to both environmental problems and the loss of liberty.

Within this story line are a number of representative characters: good scientists and bad scientists; ideologically fashionable but inept government bureaucrats whom he says have adopted biocentrism as a management philosophy; four classes of environmentalists: the trendy superrich who fund the environmental movement through their tax-exempt foundations; arrogant and dogmatic professional lobbyists in Washington, D.C. (who disagree with Chase's view of the world); the well-intended but duped middle-class rank-and-file environmentalists; and scruffy, irreverent radicals — all of whom cling to the dangerous ideology. There are also big bad timber corporations (Maxxam) and good little timber corporations (PALCO), as well as victimized rural loggers and business owners. Surrounding all these actors is the ill-informed and confused general public, seeking truth and intellectual security in a postmodern world — a half-frightened people easily detoured by false prophets. Finally, above everything, stands the philosopher.

Chase's "good" scientists have the same characteristics that Schiff imputes to virtually all scientists: they have no political agenda and, in Aaron Wildavsky's beautiful phrase, they "speak truth to power." Chase's bad scientists speak falsehood and fail to recognize the error of their theories because they are either intellectually inept or they are ideologues dressed up like scientists. Environmentalists are all converts to the false doctrine of biocentrism, and because of their quasi-religious dedication to this ideology, they are unmoved by the truth — indeed, they try to suppress it.

One class of companies in the timber industry is dedicated to sustained yield and community stability — and even supposedly achieved it before environmental and bureaucratic meddlers arrived. Another class of companies are sleazy, bottom-line raiders (Hurwitz) who are almost but not quite as bad as the ideologically impure. The local loggers and business owners appear as common heroes fighting to save their way of life, defending a rough, pioneer kind of liberal humanism.

Apart from the fray and serving as oracle and guide are the philosophers, what Chase calls "the men of ideas," including presumably, though not explicitly, himself. His view of the importance of ideas is reiterated throughout the book in key phrases and epigrams. The book opens with an epigram from John Maynard Keynes: "Ideas shape the course of history." And it closes melodramatically with the phrase, "Ideas are immortal." Perhaps most revealing of Chase's view of human nature is the epigram he uses to open the section of the book on environmental activism: "Note this, you proud men of action. You are nothing but the unconscious hodmen of the men of ideas."[7]

Chase's "hodmen" metaphor recalls Worster's herd and Schiff's mob; each is similar but each takes a slightly different view of the human nature of this familiar but incredibly ambiguous entity we call "the people." For Worster, the herd follows whomever offers material comforts and security. His is a materially based analysis of human motivation. For Schiff, the mob is simply inertial, conforming to whatever behaviors authorities can persuade them of (within reason, of course) and then cleaving to that until some new evangelical policy campaign convinces them to adopt a different behavior. For Chase, the hodmen are proud but deluded activists. Believing themselves masters of their social labor, they are actually servants of the intellectual elite. Their pride in their accomplishments blinds them to fact that they are slaves of inherited ideas promulgated by the high priests of culture.

What none of these narratives explains — or can explain — is exactly who constitutes these undifferentiated masses. The stories of real people in history never conform to such simple generalizations. I would suggest that herd, mob, and hodmen motifs are primarily narrative devices designed to explain some aspect of the relationship between actors with agency and those without it. Sometimes they simply serve as a lump-all category that includes everybody not otherwise identified in the narrative. The category is slippery, yet somehow compelling — it represents a whole in contrast to the parts usually focused on in a narrative. We can never satisfactorily characterize the whole, yet we often feel it has some reality nevertheless — like an ecosystem that cannot be delineated or bounded but that seems to have some holistic, systemic character that can be identified.

To leave out a discussion of the experience and influence of the masses on events would be elitist, yet to put them into the narrative seems reductionist. Moreover, to break the masses into all their constituent parts would add a daunting level of complexity (and perhaps redundancy) to the narrative. What to do? Try to finesse a balance between inclusion and exclusion.

In terms of inclusion, Chase's narrative is far superior to Schiff's. Not only are there more categories of actors taking part in the drama, but most categories are further broken into subcategories, as in the case of environmentalists. This provides a more accurate picture of the situation. The problem with this narrative is that its actors remain one-dimensional. There is no ambiguity of motivation, no mixture of altruism and venality in the same group, little growth or change in the players over time — the things that make humans human. The actors are all straw dogs, serving as not much more than metaphors for Chase's parable of crisis and salvation.

One lesson here, I believe, is this: the more a historian writes his or her ideological agenda into the narrative, the more artificial the actors become. They have to be portrayed in such a way that the story line is consistently reinforced. Equivocation or contradiction appears to the author as weakening the argument — just as it often appears so to readers. Now, before we become smug about the importance of "objectivity" in historical analysis, let me say that I question the validity of the concept itself. I think it is manifestly impossible to eliminate one's perspective, values, and biases from a historical narrative. It is impossible *not* to erase some actors, privilege others, and generalize about their beliefs and motivations. Once again, finding a balance between one's narrative strategy and one's desire to be "accurate" is what makes good history.

There are a couple of other interesting implications about human nature in Chase's story worth commenting on. If an erroneous idea (balance of nature, biocentrism) is the source of northwest forest problems, then the solution is to refute and replace that idea, which is exactly what Chase attempts in his lengthy tome. Not only is the full complexity of human motivations erased from this story line, but so is the material (economic) basis of natural resource decision making. Does anyone really think that all would be well in our woods if only biocentric thinking could be stamped out?

Chase shows himself to be a philosophical idealist when he argues that be-havior follows belief, in contrast to a materialist, who would argue that ideol-ogy reflects material relations. Regardless of which comes first, however, in human nature what one believes and how one behaves are not always in sync. There is no clear, consistent causal relation, yet we imply such in our narra-tives. Furthermore, people often hold conflicting beliefs and values or exceed-ingly flexible definitions of behavior appropriate to their values. Remember that James Watt quite passionately insisted he was a true environmentalist.

Environmental historians fall into both the idealist and materialist camps. Many create narratives combining both perspectives, which is probably closer to the mark. Worster, for example, emphasizes the material basis of environ-mental degradation in his ubiquitous neo-Marxist critique of capitalism, but he also points to ideology in his equally ubiquitous critique of the capitalist "ethos" and his advocacy for an ecologically based communitarian ethic. Cronon, too, recognizes the economic foundation of environmental exploita-tion in all his monographs but recently published an essay titled "The Trouble with Wilderness" that adopts essentially an idealist interpretation of environ-mental problems. He oddly, and unconvincingly in this case, argues that the wilderness idea promotes an intellectual separation of humans from nature and that such "dualistic" thinking is at the source of modern exploitative attitudes toward nature, and therefore wilderness advocacy paradoxically contributes to our environmental problems. The way to make a significant contribution to environmental protection, he suggests, is to abandon the idea of wilderness preservation as we know it. Alston Chase himself would be hard-pressed to top that view of the influence of ideas on environmental prob-lems and solutions. Cronon's exercise in semantics erases the whole political dimension of wilderness preservation and ignores the material basis of en-vironmental degradation. But I digress. . . .

A recent study combining materialist and idealist approaches and offering a rich panoply of actors with a complex set of motivations is Nancy Langston's *Forest Dreams, Forest Nightmares.*[8] It is a paradigm of problem-oriented environmental history analysis. On the first page of her introduction, Lang-ston opens with a description of a bucolic scene in the inland Northwest in the mid-nineteenth century, where pioneers found "a land of lovely open forests full of yellow-bellied ponderosa pines five feet across" (3). But then the scene changes dramatically: "After a century of trying to manage the forests, what had seemed like paradise was irrevocably lost. The great ponderosa pines had vanished, and in their place were thickets of fir trees. . . . As firs invaded the old pine forests, insect epidemics spread throughout the dry western forests. By 1991, on the five and a half million acres of Forest Service lands in the Blue

Mountains, insects had attacked half the forest stands, and in some stands nearly 70 percent of the trees were infested" (3). Destructive fires in the fir forests compounded the problem, stimulating a volatile debate over what became known as the "forest health crisis" in the inland Northwest. Langston tries to tell her readers what happened and who or what was to blame.

To do this, she had to deal first with the question of causation. Was the problem human generated or "natural" or a combination? If it was natural, then people are off the hook, so to speak, and human nature becomes a minor issue in the narrative. If the problem derived from human actions, then humans must bear responsibility and consequently human intentions, institutions, and ideologies become central to the story. Langston eschews a simple causal analysis by arguing that the undesirable environmental changes were both human generated *and* natural. In fact, she repeatedly and consciously blurs the boundary between people and nature. Nevertheless, she maintains that the *style and intensity* of logging, grazing, and fire suppression after white settlement triggered environmental changes that then escalated out of human control — changes that were essentially "natural" responses to the new mode of human occupation. Thus humans remain largely at fault for the "problems" they now face and must accept responsibility for ecological restoration, but it is not a simple "humans destroyed nature" kind of narrative.

Having established human responsibility, Langston then proceeds to delineate who exactly was at fault and why. Amidst a complicated tale of ecological transformation, human actors appear in her story in various guises and responsible in varying degrees for the undesirable changes taking place in the forests. Her story includes no villains or heroes (like Alston Chase, only she is more successful at it than he). Instead we read about (1) well-meaning but misguided foresters confused by the ecosystems they confronted, (2) a cast of pioneers holding fast to naive notions of abundance and rights of dominion, (3) a special class of scientists and silviculturists blinded by hubris into believing nature can be engineered to efficiently maximize the production of goods and services, and (4) the influential but rather impersonal force of the market that sometimes overwhelmed the better judgment of forest managers.

Other than the last actor, which hardly qualifies for the label, Langston defines the source of problems as primarily ideological: faulty ideas, simple and inadequate theories about complex forests, misunderstanding, ignorance, hubris. "It is a tragedy," she says, "in which decent people with the best of intentions destroyed what they cared for most" (6). Later in the book she says, "When foresters first arrived in the Blues they looked upon millions of acres filled with millions of trees, and every tree was different and every acre of land was different too. *Nobody had any real idea what was going on* [emphasis added (like historians approaching a body of evidence!)]. Foresters seized on simple ecological theories — in particular, succession and competition theory — as a way of reducing the mass of potential information to something they could hope to manage" (122–123). It is these faulty theories that are a prime source of difficulties later.

In another place Langston concludes, "Foresters got in trouble not because they were greedy, but because they were absolutely certain it was their mission to save the forest from its enemies. . . . Yet their enthusiasm and faith made it difficult for them to see what was going wrong" (10). Here foresters appear well intentioned but suffering from a failure of vision. This largely removes culpability from the very group of men she says were responsible for destroying the ecological communities they valued. Especially interesting here is the fine distinction she makes between "enthusiasm" and "hubris," the former being a laudable trait and the latter being a major source of ecological problems. On the one hand, early foresters approached their mission, she says, with "an exuberant faith and optimism . . . that is extremely moving" (115). On the other hand, she says, "Their very enthusiasm and faith — qualities that made them extremely effective — fostered an arrogance that often blinded them to the consequences of their actions" (98). The fine line between faith and arrogance corresponds exactly to the fine line between innocence and culpability. How to distinguish the two is the challenge.

As her assessment of the psychology of foresters becomes more subtle, her explanation of the cause of forest problems and her assignment of culpability grows correspondingly more obscure. This obscurity is compounded when she finally acknowledges some of the material forces responsible for environmental degradation. Her statement that market forces "overwhelmed" the better judgment of foresters moves us even further from being able to blame faulty ideas and misunderstanding. This impersonal force of the market then becomes the culprit rather than the actual decision makers in the Forest Service who supposedly knew what should have been done. Their better judgment remained intact, she implies, but could not withstand the external pressures of the market.

This is a substantially more complicated and ambiguous tale than Schiff and Chase offer. The character and motivation of Langston's scientists are as hard to pin down as the question of culpability. They are heroes, yet they ruined the forests. And they ruined them not because they were greedy or captured by industry but because they tried to save and later improve the forests. In one passage the early foresters appear as gifted naturalists and skilled observers seeking knowledge; in the next passage they are frightened by the strangeness that surrounds them and goaded by their ignorance into adopting simple explanatory theories that don't fit the context. When the railroads come to the Blues, bringing access to markets with them, the foresters go to battle against the timber corporations one day and then turn around and promote big timber sales to the big companies at the expense of the small local mills the next day. As the foresters tried to do the right thing, all the wrong things resulted.

Thus Langston offers an assessment of cause and effect that is difficult to sort out, and that difficulty, I suggest, is directly tied to the complexity of her analysis. No one appears blatantly culpable, and no one class of actors seems in control of events. In fact, no one seems to be in charge at all (unlike the narratives of Worster, Chase, and Schiff); not even nature itself seems in control, although Langston's portrayal of nature's effective resistance to management makes humans appear rather small and ineffectual in the narrative. It's an interesting finesse: she convinces us that human actions have dramatically altered the inland northwest landscape but that humans have never really been in control of those alterations, that ecological change proceeded on an uncharted and entirely unintended path despite vigorous attempts to direct forest change.

As in any good problem-oriented analysis, Langston also addresses the issue of solutions. The solution she offers follows in lockstep what she sees as the main source of the problem: better knowledge, humility, a change in values, and for the narrative inclined: "a new set of stories about the relationship between wild forests and people." In a chapter titled "Restoring the Inland West" she says, "At the root of our problems with managing land is fragmentation, both ecological and ethical. Our forests are fragmented, and so are we. We live like little islands cut off from the places we inhabit" (10). What is the way out of this condition? "Fragmentation is a spiritual state," she continues, "a moral state of disconnection. . . . Removing this fragmentation between human and nature means moving away from seeing nature as something we can fragment into commodities and resources." We need to adopt an ethic of "attentive humility rather than an ethic of control" (280).

What is too often missing in her description of the "problem" is a material explanation for human motives and actions. What is too often missing from her solution is the institutional restructuring necessary to alter the way power, wealth, and decision making are presently configured. People seem primarily driven by ideas and ideals, so that incorrect conceptions of nature lead to environmental problems, while correct conceptions of nature will resolve them — similar to Cronon's thesis in "The Trouble with Wilderness" or like Alston Chase, though quite a bit more ecologically sophisticated and gratefully lacking Chase's simplistic conspiracy theories.

The emphasis on the mind of the scientist in Langston's narrative is perhaps explained by the fact that Langston herself spent some years as a scientist (before she got her Ph.D. in history). She admits she is interested primarily in what makes foresters tick, but I think that interest causes her to exaggerate the role of the foresters and of the ecological paradigms they labored under.

So, what can we conclude from all this? First, all narratives are reductionist. Problem-oriented narratives in particular reduce the field of all possible historical participants to those relevant to a discussion of the problem and its solution. This involves a process of lumping and splitting, privileging and erasing. We cannot avoid this and should not be ashamed of it, but we should at least be cognizant of it and willing to discuss it openly. Second, fewer actors makes for a cleaner story line but a less intellectually satisfying one and less useful for explaining historical events. A complicated panoply of actors lends sophistication to a narrative but is harder to orchestrate, and taken too far, it can repel an audience. Treading that fine line is an art. Third, the author's story line and narrative strategy constrain how human actors are portrayed. If the tale is a battle between good and evil, justice and corruption, altruism and greed, then actors will be drawn to represent those traits. Two-dimensional plots with one-dimensional characters in concise relationships make simple dramatic tales that unfortunately often have wide appeal (notice my own derogatory reference here to the nature of the masses!). Complex stories, with characters that exhibit all the ambiguity and contradictions we ourselves exhibit, can be powerful and compelling if told effectively, or they can seem unfocused and unconvincing. Once again, finding a balance is the art of historical writing.

Ultimately, as Cronon argues in "A Place for Stories," historical narratives are tales, with a plot line and a moral, a special form of communication with a pedagogical intent. Environmental historians have gone a long way toward getting the profession to stop taking nature for granted and to accept it as a legitimate multidimensional "actor" in the historical drama. It is important, however, for we environmental historians to remember that human nature cannot be taken for granted either.

NOTES

1. Donald Worster, *Rivers of Empire: Water, Aridity, and the Growth of the American West* (New York: Pantheon, 1985), 57–58.
2. Ashley L. Schiff, *Fire and Water: Scientific Heresy in the Forest Service* (Cambridge: Harvard University Press, 1962).
3. Ibid., chapter 2.
4. Ibid., 167.

5. Alston Chase, *In a Dark Wood: The Fight Over Forests and the Rising Tyranny of Ecology* (New York: Houghton Mifflin, 1995).

6. Ibid., xiii.

7. Ibid., 177. A hod is a tray for carrying mortar, and a hodman carries bricks and mortar for the bricklayer.

8. Nancy Langston, *Forest Dreams, Forest Nightmares: The Paradox of Old Growth in the Inland West* (Seattle: University of Washington Press, 1995). Subsequent references to *Forest Dreams* are given in parentheses in the text.

CHAPTER EIGHT

HUMAN NATURE
IN THE VAULT

Andrew Kirk

The collection and preservation of an authentic domain of identity cannot be natural or innocent. It is tied up with nationalistic politics, with restrictive law, and with contested encodings of past and future.
— JAMES CLIFFORD, *The Predicament of Culture*

THE PLACE

If you look at the city of Denver from the air, you can't help noticing the clean lines and swaths of green radiating out from the center of the metropolis. From the brown prairie, wide parkways lead the visitor to the "Queen City of the Plains," an urban oasis on the edge of the Rocky Mountains. All spokes take one toward the crowning glory of Denver's "City Beautiful" movement: Civic Center Park. Lavish flower beds, towering hardwood trees, and monumental statuary announce your arrival into a "natural" space carved out of the heart of downtown. Businessmen, weary politicians, and office workers find solace from the vicissitudes of the white-collar jungle in this peaceful garden. Surrounding this well-ordered landscape stands a collection of massive neoclassical buildings housing the offices of government for the city and the state. The theme of the architecture is unmistakable — progress and enlightenment. Amidst these hulking replicas of ancient splendor, two singular structures catch the modern observer's eye. The Denver Museum of Art is a towering monument to modernism. Gray ceramic tiles reflect the sun and highlight a profusion of seemingly random windows. No less startling is the whimsical facade of the Denver Public Library, recently completed at a cost to the taxpayers of $65 million. Consisting of towers of native stone crowned by an unlikely copper mortarboard large enough to land a Huey chopper, the library screams for attention. Like the neoclassical buildings that surround it, the library is a product of its time, a postmodern dream or nightmare, depending on who you talk to, embodying the idea of organized chaos.

The subject of this essay is the Conservation Library, an archival collection contained within the Denver Public Library system. In many respects the history of this obscure little place illuminates the zeitgeist of an era, and the evolution and persistence of ideas of human nature in environmental politics. The postwar period in American history has been defined, to a certain extent, by changing ideas about the relationship between humans and the nonhuman environment. Baby boomers, for example, began to reject the consumerism of the 1950s as notions of ecology, conservation, and preservation filtered into popular political discourse. The Progressive idea of perpetual growth and linear progress through technological development and scientific management lost much of its currency during the 1960s. Older leaders of the conservation movement faced the difficult task of reconciling their Progressive faith in the system with an increasingly radical critique from younger members of a complex and rapidly changing environmental coalition. In addition, like the leaders of the civil rights movement, established conservationists also faced a challenge from within as women demanded a voice in policymaking and leadership. The evolution of the Conservation Library reflected and influenced these changes and conflicts. In many ways the story of the library and the environmental movement is a story of social change and painful ideological reorientation. At the Conservation Library, advocacy on behalf of the nonhuman environment became the backdrop for profound changes in the way humans dealt with other humans, and ideas about human nature played a key role in this process.

In the spring of 1995 the Denver Public Library opened its newly constructed main branch in downtown Denver. Designed by Michael Graves, an architect known for creating interesting and controversial buildings, the building of the new structure generated a lot of local interest. The regional press closely covered the construction, and the grand opening became front-page news. Upon my arrival in Denver, to spend the summer researching in the collections of the Conservation Library, friends besieged me with requests to tour the infamous new structure. About twice a week throughout the summer I led a tour through the building, becoming so familiar with the architecture, art, and history of the place that I began to feel like a docent.

My tour of this iconoclastic structure began, quite naturally, at the main entrance. Here just beyond a steamy hot dog stand, run by recent Russian immigrants, a towering portico leads Lilliputian visitors from the noise and confusion of downtown streets into the quiet grandeur of the entrance hall. The library is at once an ordinary place where homeless people methodically flip through the pages of magazines trying to stay warm and a mysterious place full of remarkable relics and forgotten stories. The cool marble of the entry hall leads visitors toward a bank of stainless steel elevators. Groups of rowdy schoolchildren trip over each other as the elevator empties in preparation for another trip from the public space of the lobby to the rarefied atmosphere of the upper research floors. Stepping out onto the fifth floor — home of the famed Western History Collection — library patrons find themselves suddenly and unexpectedly in a sacred space. Cold steel and high ceilings give way to warm woods, dim lights, and rooms of a more human scale. The first thing one notices as the elevator doors slide closed is Albert Bierstadt's monumental painting *Estes Park — The Rocky Mountains*. The juxtaposition of late-twentieth-century modern architecture and grand nineteenth-century romantic landscape painting never fails to startle the unsuspecting visitor. A window on the wilderness, the painting provides the entry point into a world of preserved nature — a "vault" where visitors can view the relics of the conservation movement and in so doing reevaluate their culture of consumption and reconstruct their view of nature in the heart of the city.

This essay is a brief meditation on the Conservation Library that raises and tries to answer a set of questions about the efforts of a small yet influential group of environmental thinkers to construct a monument to themselves and their philosophy, and the ways these efforts reflect some basic assumptions about nature and human nature in environmental discourse. Why did this unusual place come into being when and where it did? Why, in the 1960s, did many of the leaders of the American environmental movement work so diligently to create a physical space to house their ideas? But most of all, in what ways does the creation of this place reveal how notions of human nature have structured modern environmentalism?

THE IDEA

On the fifth floor of the Denver Public Library, just beyond the Bierstadt painting, lie the collections of the Conservation Library, a world of material objects representing the dream of preserving the romantic wilderness depicted on Bierstadt's canvas. Gradually, as the visitor walks through the rooms of the fifth floor, a story unfolds. The history of environmental thinking in America takes form in stately rows of books, stacks of manuscripts, paintings, and jumbles of artifacts. Restoration of the human spirit through contact with wilderness, the central ideal of the conservation movement, is embodied in Arthur Carhart's Conservation Library Collection (CLC), the once beloved but now forlorn stepchild of the western history department. Growing out of Carhart's personal collections—gathered during a forty-year career as a Forest Service land planner and conservation author—the CLC came to represent an attempt, in the 1950s and 1960s, to preserve a particular vision of the American environment and educate a new generation of environmental advocates. This vision encompassed fears about dwindling natural resources, overpopulation, and technocracy. In addition to concerns about the state of the earth, Carhart and his cohorts worried about the state of human nature in a postatomic world.

The founders of the CLC sought to reify their ideology in physical space and recapture their visions of nature and a simpler society in a place open to the greatest number of people: a public library. Like a skid-row rescue mission with a flickering neon cross, the Conservation Library stood as a beacon of light in the dark heart of the city. Here, it was hoped, a generation could be redeemed and returned to the fold, cured of "unnatural" modern behaviors that led to environmental ignorance and ultimately to cultural decay. For Carhart and his peers, the surge of emotion inspired by "nature" was so profound that they believed it to be something characteristically human. Individuals who did not share their love of the wilderness and the nonhuman world clearly suffered, in their view, from a type of false consciousness or, more cynically, were the products of an inferior background. Their middle-class attitudes toward the natural world were, they thought, the only legitimate position. The early mission of the CLC was to enlighten the public, helping ordinary people reawaken their innate connections with the natural world through contact with carefully selected artifacts, books, and displays. This selection process involved environmentalists from many different organizations across the country under the direction of the irrepressible Art Carhart.

Raised on a steady diet of science, the young Carhart strove to bring modern scientific methods to bear on his hobbies and work. An ornithologist and hunter by avocation and landscape architect and writer by trade, he spent his youth immersed in natural history, publishing his first article, a study of the woolly owl, at age eleven. During the 1950s, however, he found himself increasingly alienated from the world of modern atomic science and postwar technology. Like Henry Adams a generation before him, Carhart worried about the growing conflict between the technological and the sublime—the dynamo and the virgin. A lifelong Progressive, by the late 1950s Carhart began to question contemporary ideas of progress and modernity. He worried particularly about the consequences of technocratic thinking for American society and culture. To some extent Carhart shared, with many of his contemporaries in the conservation movement, a set of ideas most easily described as "antimodernism."

Antimodernism has been defined by historian Jackson Lears as "a feeling of revulsion with the banality and weightlessness of modern post-industrial life."[1] This definition nicely fits the rising tide of emotion that drove an eclectic group of individuals and organizations to build the Conservation Library in 1960. Central to the antimodernist alienation from the postwar world was a fear that the prominence of the hard sciences, the expansion of the space race, and the expansion of consumer technology deemphasized contact with the nonhuman world. The idea of a generation of Americans who no longer needed to spend time fishing, hunting, climbing, or even picnicking horrified Carhart and his friends.[2]

Although deeply concerned about modern life, Carhart, like most of his peers in the conservation movement, choose to live in the city and enjoy the material advantages of the postwar economic boom and the rise of the consumer culture. The construction of the Conservation Library became entwined in the tension between the modern and the antimodern. The ambivalence in Carhart's early proposals for the CLC reflected the general ambivalence of Americans toward preservation and development. "I suppose I am a typical American," he once wrote, a statement supported by the pull he felt between the modern world he lived in and enjoyed and the wilderness world he worked in and loved.[3]

Carhart was not alone in his fears of the modern world: a growing number of people in his generation, along with millions of baby boomers, were equally concerned. Not only afraid of pesticides and atomic bombs, they were in many respects afraid of each other.

At the root of these anxieties were some fundamental assumptions about human nature. In the first place, Carhart thought that all persons possessed "a few *universal* human traits—such homely attributes as individual selfishness, a tendency toward laziness . . . [and] an equally fundamental acquisitiveness."[4] Only through wilderness experiences could these natural tendencies be dulled, forcing people to live in harmony with their human community and the natural world. Not surprisingly city dwellers, especially young people, elicited the most concern. Trapped in what Carhart called the "metropolitan straight-jacket," Americans began to exhibit pronounced antisocial behavior such as "tossing garbage and litter" and even "yelling and running" through picnic spots with little regard for the rights of the nature lover trying to enjoy a quiet afternoon in contemplation of the sublime.[5]

Ironically, human tendencies toward *wild* and chaotic behavior could, in

Carhart's philosophy, only be subdued by contact with lands and creatures perceived as equally *wild*. As he stated in 1960, "Self-discipline is learned best in surroundings other than the strictly regulated city."[6] In summarizing his position on the preservation of wilderness later that same year, Carhart stated, "If there is one lesson sojourning in the wildlands can teach it is the individual's responsibility to the community."[7] The rowdy youths who vandalized the parks around Carhart's home were, he thought, a product of the urban consumer culture of the 1950s. Carhart wanted to take these "rebels without a cause" out of their confining urban environment and convert them into useful and productive citizens in the sanctuary of the wilderness. The problem for Carhart and those who felt like he did was how to get the ever expanding hoards of baby boomers into the wild. No less significant was the question of what would happen to the wilderness if millions of baby boomers actually *did* heed his call and trample en masse through the mountains and forests.

For Carhart and the middle-class men and women of the conservation community, the only legitimate way to know the natural world was through recreation. Only the "intense experience" of wilderness recreation could banish the banality and turmoil of the modern world. They considered hunting, fishing, bird watching, mountaineering, hiking, and picnicking the most acceptable pursuits. By the early 1960s Carhart had spent more than forty years preaching the gospel of wilderness recreation. Hired by the Forest Service as their first landscape architect in 1919, he almost single-handedly legitimized the idea of recreation as part of the service's multiple-use mission. Between 1920 and 1950 he saw his dreams of forest recreation become a reality. At the same time he and his generation of conservationists began to worry that their work was fading from public view. Although the number of wilderness visitors increased with each passing year, Carhart thought that too many of the new visitors merely sped through the forests in their cars, rarely stopping long enough to have a *real* wilderness experience.

The solution to this problem came to Carhart one afternoon as he sat contemplating the mountains of nature literature, field notes, wilderness photos, and hunting trophies that cluttered the basement of his Denver home. If you can't bring the people to the wilderness, he thought, then bring the wilderness to the people. As an avid collector of anything and everything related to the outdoors, Carhart began thinking of how to use his vast personal papers and trophies as tools to instruct people, especially young people, about his wilderness philosophies. Gradually he envisioned a research archive where his prized possessions could reside along with other artifacts gathered from around the globe; it would be a sanctuary that provided a home for nature within the confines of the city, a place of instruction where people "blinded by the fearful brightness of the atomic bomb, [and] the winking of traffic lights,"[8] could experience vicariously the wildlands and subdue their innate tendencies toward self-destruction. With this goal in mind, Carhart began collecting in earnest. Enlisting the help of the national conservation and wilderness recreation community, he collected artifacts and documents representing the past history of the conservation movement and the effort to preserve wilderness in America. He also solicited any type of material representing the elements of the environment most likely to elicit a reverence for outdoor life to urban viewers unfamiliar with the benefits of the strenuous life.

If Carhart had not pursued a career as an author and conservationist, he would have made an exceptional salesman. He possessed a knack for converting people to his causes, and the idea for the Conservation Library was no different. In a matter of days after his revelation, Carhart had contacted some forty leaders of the national conservation movement to solicit contributions and support. Later that same week he managed to convince Denver city librarian John Eastlick that the library system should sponsor the cause and donate space to house the collections. Carhart's apocalyptic predictions and fiery rhetoric convinced the conservative Eastlick, who then sold the idea to the city council. Eastlick proved to be a key ally for Carhart. He experienced a personal conversion to the conservation cause and became a dedicated supporter of Carhart's efforts to educate the public about the benefits of wilderness experience as a corrective to the limitations of human nature. Other prominent leaders of the rapidly expanding American environmental movement became equally convinced that the development of a research archive was the key to successful advocacy in the future.

Cultural theorist James Clifford has commented, "Collecting has long been [used as] a strategy for the deployment of a possessive self, culture, and authenticity."[9] In assembling the artifacts of the Conservation Library the leaders of the environmental movement sought to create a physical sanctuary where familiar objects might provide an antidote to their neo-Malthusian fears and *Doctor Strangelove* nightmares. Carhart's notions of human nature fueled the collecting process and shaped the growing library.

The Conservation Library was never intended to be a museum with a primary focus on material artifacts. Nonetheless, the place that evolved was more akin to what we might think of as a museum collection than to a traditional library manuscript collection. In choosing the medium of collection and display of material culture, the founders of the CLC tapped into a long tradition in western cultures. For centuries collectors used the material they assembled to "celebrate the stability of their belief systems" while educating the public about their social and political philosophies.[10] Collections are, above all, the careful ordering of space to create a semblance of order in a chaotic world. The creators of the CLC assumed that the material they assembled was significant and intrinsically meaningful and that somehow the whole, a collection of conservation-related things, was greater than the sum of its parts. It was therefore worth spending time and money to preserve the collection as a distinct body with an autonomous physical location.

Despite their antimodernist leanings and sharp criticisms of modern industrial life and society, the founders of the CLC shared with most of their middle-class contemporaries an underlying belief in a modernist metanarrative with comprehensible objective truths, indisputable facts, and a patina of scientific legitimacy. In their view, human reason, given the time and proper instruction and tamed by strenuous activity away from centers of humanity, could define and explain an objective reality. Following this logic, the CLC, as a repository for the primary evidence in the search for truth, could help enlighten the masses and get society back on track.[11] With these goals in mind Carhart set about building his center in the fall of 1960, and by the spring of 1961 it was ready for its public debut.

BRIEF HISTORY

At the newly opened CLC the story of the preservation of wilderness untrammeled began, ironically, in a locked temperature-controlled room of decidedly human artifacts. Guests at the official grand opening, including conservation dignitaries and CLC supporters like David Brower and Howard Zahniser, flew in to view the relics and peruse the manuscripts. Curious library patrons followed the crowds to the fourth floor, where they passed through two large frosted glass doors, emblazoned with the CLC's new icon. Tall oak cabinets and bookshelves with wire mesh doors contained conservation treasures from around the country. Every corner overflowed with archive boxes, trunks, and sacks of manuscripts. Wrought-iron gates led into the rare-book room. The prize possession, Howard Zahniser's personal book collection carefully cataloged and lovingly displayed, occupied the center of the room. Next to the Zahniser books visitors could sort through a jumble of material artifacts. From the dusty shadows a marble bust of William Gilpin, former Colorado governor and leading proponent of the "rain follows the plow" idea, locked startled visitors in his stony gaze; an unusual icon for an environmental collection. Next to Gilpin sat John Muir's glasses displayed alongside a small wooden box holding a presidential fountain pen used to sign the law protecting the American bison. A central case housed another of the library's prized possessions, Aldo Leopold's field notes and an early manuscript for *A Sand County Almanac* illuminated with margin notes and pencil illustrations. In the corner of the room on that festive night one might find groups of conservationists gathered around reel-to-reel tape players, listening to the recorded voices of elderly forest rangers recounting the glory days of the Forest Service.

Among the oddest artifacts in the vault of the Conservation Library was the great seal of the Ladies Auxiliary of the Colorado KKK. What could such a thing be doing in such a place? What linked attempts to preserve race and sex purity with the drive to preserve the American wilderness?[12] Although I don't want to suggest that Carhart and the founders of the CLC shared the goals of the KKK, there are some interesting parallels. Like the women of the KKK, very active in Colorado during the 1920s, Carhart and his peers fearfully viewed changes in American culture and values during a period of prosperity and growth. In addition, both groups responded to demographic changes that appeared to shift the power balance toward groups they feared. By the late 1950s Carhart and many of the older leaders of the conservation movement became increasingly concerned with the population explosion of the postwar years. Educating the public about the environmental consequences of overpopulation became one of the central goals of the library in the early 1960s.

Neo-Malthusian fears raised the question among the founders of the library of how *many* people are good or bad for "nature" and, of course, *who* the good or bad people are. A key figure in influencing the library's population control philosophy was CLC adviser and national executive secretary of Planned Parenthood William Vogt. In the dawning days of the baby boom Vogt argued in his influential and widely read book *Road to Survival,* "We support as public charges . . . the senile, the incurables, the insane, the paupers, and those who might be called ecological incompetents, such as the subsidized stockmen and sheepherders. They exist to [destroy] the means of national survival . . . [and are] the source of environmental sickness."[13] Carhart expanded Vogt's categories to include the rapidly swelling urban youth population along with other urban victims of unrestrained human nature as a part of the growing population of "ecological incompetents."

The ideas of human nature evident in the early founding of the CLC reflected philosophies of the environmental movement as a whole. The accepted mode of communion with nature involved recreational experiences and wilderness. Carhart viewed people who used the wilderness for recreation as healthy members of society. On the other hand, those who advocated the destruction or sale of wilderness got lumped with the "senile" and the "insane" individuals clearly not masters of their own nature. One of the central insights Carhart contributed to the environmental movement in the early 1960s was the notion that sportsmen and moderate resource managers played a key role in successful environmental coalitions. The failure to welcome all who participated in outdoor recreation into the conservation fold, Carhart feared, risked relinquishing power to the "ecological incompetents." Unfortunately Carhart's pleas for accommodation and compromise often fell on deaf ears. Many environmentalists of the early 1960s began to question the role of sportsmen and other individuals and organizations that supported a less than pure vision of wilderness preservation. For a time, this ideology posed no serious threat either to the rapidly expanding library or to the environmental movement.

The publication of Rachel Carson's *Silent Spring* helped crystallize the ecological thinking of a generation, spawning the modern environmental movement and starting what writer Kirkpatrick Sale has aptly identified as a "Green Revolution."[14] Three years after the founding of the CLC a broad coalition of individuals and institutions came together to successfully support the federal Wilderness Bill in 1964, culminating decades of grassroots advocacy. By the mid-1960s it seemed that the future of environmental advocacy, and the CLC as the main archive for the movement, would only brighten with the passing years. To a certain extent this was true. In the wake of *Silent Spring* and the Wilderness Act a wave of environmentalism swept the nation, culminating with Earth Day and the popular explosion of ecological thinking in the 1970s. The Conservation Library stood poised to become a major center of environmental activism at the dawn of the environmental age.

Beneath the surface of optimism and hope, however, conflict was brewing. Legal fights over expanding wilderness and conflict between grassroots groups and larger national groups began to surface. In addition anti-environmental groups began to organize on a grassroots level and use the environmentalists' own tactics to wage battles over the federal lands in the American West, sometimes mobilizing constituencies that had supported the 1964 Wilderness Bill. Also a younger cohort of more radical environmentalists, spearheaded by animal-rights activists, began to view hunters and sportsmen as enemies instead of potential allies. By the early 1980s the competing sides of land use and environmental protection were more entrenched and polarized than ever.

Tensions within the movement also escalated as generation conflicts over counterculture influences created entrenched factions. Most significantly, many young environmentalists began to move away from the technophobia of Carhart and his generation and looked to new technologies, especially in the area of government-sponsored energy and information development, as useful and good. Divisions within the Conservation Library reflected these trends. Ideological disagreements caused strain between the directors of the CLC and the Denver Public Library board, ultimately leading to the alienation of more conservative supporters, who withdrew both their moral and financial support.

Part of the problem for the CLC and the national environmental movement stemmed from unacknowledged notions of human nature. The idea that nature, particularly wilderness, existed as a safety valve for innate human failings fueled the founding of the CLC and the passage of the Wilderness Act. Carhart and his contemporaries were as concerned with the shape and future of human society and particularly with the safety of the middle-class life they had become accustomed to as they were about the natural world. In their zealous rhetoric about population, *good* and *bad* people, the value of wilderness and the *re-creation* of the human spirit, Carhart's successors at the CLC and environmentalists in general often lost sight of economic and social reality. People who labored in nature, particularly ranchers, loggers, and miners, became enemies of the cause. This had not been the case, or at least not to the same degree, in the 1950s and early 1960s. The original coalition that came together to support and fund the Conservation Library had been diverse, including members of the resource business community. In fact, diversity was critical to the early success of the library. In order to survive within the public bureaucracy of the Denver Public Library system, the CLC needed to at least appear to be politically neutral, with support from a cross section of the public. A growing distrust of labor and alternatives to the original middle-class program began by the mid-1970s to undermine the library's support. As Richard White has argued, "By failing to examine and claim work within nature, environmentalists have ceded to the so-called wise-use movement valuable cultural terrain."[15] For the Conservation Library the price of the failure to modify their rigid vision of nature and human nature was left to be paid by the next generation.

This new generation raised more money and garnered more support than Carhart dreamed possible. They also dramatically expanded the audience for the library by making the most of cutting-edge information technology and moving far away from the anti-modernism and human nature philosophy of their predecessors. Despite this success the CLC became a victim of the Reagan revolution. Federal, state, and city funds disappeared, forcing the CLC to close its doors to the public in 1982. The artifacts and manuscript collections were boxed up and carted off to a warehouse in lower downtown Denver. The once celebrated holdings of the CLC, visited by environmental leaders and researchers from around the globe, became the home to generations of mice — the only visitors homeless men seeking shelter from a winter storm and the occasional graduate student searching for a dissertation topic.

BORN AGAIN

The building of the Conservation Library was an exercise in cultural construction. An examination of the landscape and rhetoric of the archives and publications of the CLC reveals the unintended consequences of the effort to envision alternatives to the materialism and technocracy of 1950s American culture. At the same time it speaks to the social tensions that shaped the environmental movement as it developed over the last four decades. Sometimes intentionally and sometimes not, Arthur Carhart and the founders of the Conservation Library used their particular vision of human nature to guide their collecting, educational, and advocacy efforts. To a small yet significant degree their actions contributed to the transformation of the American environmental movement and helped shape public discourse on environmental issues. One of the most important legacies of this place is a remarkable collection of introspective records from some of the leading figures in the environmental movement. The very public nature of the construction of the CLC forced Arthur Carhart and everyone involved in the project to explicitly define their ideology and reevaluate their ideas of nature and human nature. The process of building the Conservation Library provides a captivating glimpse into the tensions and complexities involved in constructing an environmental consciousness in a society obsessed with material progress.

In the fall of 1995, after fourteen years in limbo, the Conservation Library was reborn. In the early afternoon the newly finished Edward Hobbs Hilliard reading room fills with light. Hilliard was a friend of Carhart's and an early supporter of the CLC who was tragically killed in a mountaineering accident. In this room on shiny new selves sit the dusty volumes of the Howard Zahniser memorial book collection once again open to the public. The Hilliard room is tucked away from view in a cozy corner of the new fifth floor of the Denver Public Library. Only a small sign marks the border between the genealogy department and the remains of the Conservation Library. On any given morning you can find a small herd of elderly genealogists waiting impatiently outside the library for the doors to open. They rush up to the fifth floor, grabbing favorite microfilm machines and tables. Few ever make it to the sunny little room at the back of the building. For those who do a treasure awaits — an intellectual family tree of the American environmental movement.

NOTES

I would like to thank Virginia Scharff, Richard Etulain, Frank Szasz, John Herron, and the participants of the New Mexico Environmental Symposium for thoughtful discussions on this topic and comments on this essay. The original research for this paper was partially funded by a University of New Mexico Research and Travel Grant. Additional funding came from the Dudley Phillips Dissertation Fellowship.

1. T. J. Jackson Lears, *No Place of Grace: Antimodernism and the Transformation of American Culture, 1880–1920* (New York: Pantheon, 1981).

2. Carhart's notions of human nature are remarkably similar to those expressed by proponents of biophilia, notably E. O. Wilson, as in this quote, "What . . . will happen to the human psyche when such a defining part of the human evolutionary experience [contact with wild nature] is diminished or erased?" E. O. Wilson and Stephen R. Kellert, eds., *The Biophilia Hypothesis* (Washington, D.C.: Island Press, 1994), 35.

3. Arthur Carhart, "A Brief Biographical Sketch," Carhart Papers, box 699, DPL/WHC.

4. Arthur Carhart, "Down Went Communism," *Family Circle,* November 3, 1944, 11.

5. Arthur Carhart, *Planning for America's Wildlands* (Harrisburg, Pa.: Telegraph Press, 1961), 3.

6. Ibid., 3.

7. Ibid., 2.

8. John Eastlick, "Proposed Collection of Conservation of Natural Resources," Conservation Library Archive, box 4, f. 51, DPL/WHC.

9. James Clifford, *The Predicament of Culture: Twentieth-Century Ethnography, Literature, and Art* (Cambridge: Harvard University Press), 218.

10. David Jenkins, "Object Lessons and Ethnographic Displays: Museum Exhibitions and the Making of American Anthropology," *Comparative Studies in Society and History* 36, no. 2 (April 1994): 242.

11. Susan Pearce, *Museums, Objects, and Collections* (Washington, D.C.: Smithsonian, 1992).

12. Mary Douglas, *Purity and Danger: An Analysis of Concepts of Pollution and Taboo* (London: Routledge, 1980).

13. William Vogt, *Road to Survival* (New York: William Sloane Associates, 1948), 145.

14. Kirkpatrick Sale, *The Green Revolution: The American Environmental Movement, 1962–1992* (New York: Hill & Wang, 1993).

15. Richard White, *The Organic Machine* (New York: Hill & Wang, 1995).

AFTERWORD: A VIEW FROM ACROSS THE HALL

Problems of Delineation and
Value in Nature and Human Nature

Timothy Moy

INTRODUCTION

My office is across the hall from that of Andy Kirk and John Herron. For the better part of the year, I had the pleasure of eavesdropping on many intriguing and impromptu discussions between Andy, John, and Virginia Scharff that swirled around the difficulties of terms like *nature* and *human nature*. Eventually they must have noticed me listening in from around the doorway, because they gradually and generously drew me in to their deliberations.

Most of the conversations I consequently found myself in were framed in the language of environmental history, but as the new resident historian of science, I found these issues very relevant, and even familiar, to the history of science. I gradually took on the role of a "familiar outsider" in this discussion — a role I happily continued by moderating a postmortem round-table discussion for the New Mexico Environmental Symposium on human nature that culminated in this volume.

Like environmental historians, historians of science recognize the complexities of *nature* as historical construct. For both, nature is a construct *and* a reality. On the one hand, there can be no question that nature is constructed, with history and characteristics that vary between cultures and eras. Nature has been, at one time or another, dark and mysterious or bright and transparent; passive and harmonious or aggressive and violent, red in tooth and claw; organic and feminine or mechanical and masculine.[1] Nature is clearly a historicized category.

On the other hand, nature is reality and constrains the kinds of stories that historians can tell. No meaningful narrative in the history of science today could have gravity bending to human will or the sun and other stars orbiting earth. Likewise, no meaningful environmental history could have drought-plagued farmers conjuring water out of their imaginations or successfully irrigating their corn with dust.

It is this fascinating tension — between nature as construct and nature as reality — that drives many historiographical debates in history of science and also drove much of the discussion at the New Mexico Environmental Symposium. While the focus of the papers was on the consequences of unexamined perceptions of *human* nature, an equal amount of attention examined perceptions of nature more broadly conceived. For environmental historians, it seems to me that there are two fundamental problems that stem from unexamined or underexamined conceptions of both nature and human nature: a problem of delineation and a problem of value.

PROBLEMS FOR NATURE

The delineation problem for nature is simply this: Strictly speaking, nothing can exist outside of nature.[2] As the term has come to be used in the western world, *nature* is essentially a synonym for the entire physical universe — its substance, its energy, its laws, its phenomena. The naturalistic worldview, which rose in the seventeenth century and lies at the heart of modernism, maintains that the same "natural laws" that hold for rocks, ants, and beavers also hold for humans. Humans are part of nature; it is beyond our ability to be otherwise.

This means, of course, that nothing humans do is or can be meaningfully "unnatural." No human activity or product can belong less to nature than the actions or products of ants or beavers. All of these organisms build, destroy, consume, and produce; I can see no meaningful and coherent distinction between the works of humans and the works of anything else. In fact, it seems quite immodest to me to suggest that humans, alone among living organisms, have some unique capacity to transcend the universe from which they spring.

But simply because our actions are natural does not make them good or desirable. This is the second problem with our conception of nature — the problem of value. Despite centuries of philosophical discourse on the moral distinction between *is* and *ought,* there is still a common belief that what is natural is implicitly good or proper. By this argument, nature has bestowed moral sanction upon numerous practices — like eating meat, or aggressive or even violent behavior, or the recreational use of mood-altering chemical substances (but only naturally occurring ones — no synthetics) — because they occur in the "natural world"; that is, one or more nonhuman species has these practices in their behavioral repertoire. Conversely, other human behaviors — like homosexuality — are condemned morally on the grounds that they are somehow "unnatural," supposedly not occurring in nonhuman nature (a contention that is actually untrue in this case).

How ridiculous! The history of science in the western world is replete with examples of how this appeal to nature has been used to justify the most horrible of human actions — racism, sexism, classism, war, genocide.[3] For historical reasons alone, we should have consigned the morality of nature to the trash heap long ago.

There are obvious nonhistorical reasons for abandoning this attitude as well, and (ironically) nature itself provides them. Even a brief perusal of life on earth reveals a multitude of practices that we must consider ambiguous from a moral point of view. Many litter-bearing organisms will occasionally eat their newborn offspring. Many insects will consume their parents or their mates. Male dolphins will "herd" females; that is, forcibly seclude and probably gang-rape them. Among some chimpanzees, the dominant male (if you believe in such things) will occasionally kill a newborn chimp, forcing the recent mother back into estrus; to complete the drama, the entire clan will then gather around the dead infant and eat it.

Such examples can be multiplied at will. But if these sound like isolated and bizarre behaviors, even if "natural," it is worth remembering that the golden rule of predation is that the first targets in the ongoing struggle for survival are always the young, the sick, the old, and the infirm. Predatory animals always prefer to prey on the defenseless.

What possible moral guidelines can humans draw for themselves from such natural occurrences? It would be ludicrous to suggest, for example, that infants or mates make proper (not to mention convenient) snacks simply because other organisms find them so; waste not, want not. Sincere and serious attempts to find moral lessons in nature have usually ended up sounding quaint and tortured if not absurd. I have always felt a little sorry for mid-nineteenth-century naturalists who tried valiantly to reconcile their Victorian faith in the inherent morality of nature and the wondrous new information arriving daily from their colleagues in the field. One source of difficulty at the time involved Ichneumonoidea, wasps that begin their lives as parasites, feeding on the bodies of other insects. Parasitism is never pretty, but the practices of the ichneumons are unusually grisly. Females inject their eggs directly within the unfortunate host via an ovipositor or, after paralyzing it, lay their eggs on the host's body. In both cases, the host remains alive, better to serve as main dish in the gruesome feast that commences when the eggs hatch. Since the hungry wasp larvae would lose a great deal of potential sustenance if they killed their host right away, they display a remarkable efficiency by eating very selectively — fat and other nonessential structures first — leaving their host's more vital organs until the end. The last to go are the heart and nervous system, leaving only the hollow shell of the adult host.[4]

How could one find any sort of moral guidance in the practice of parasitically devouring a living creature from within? A prominent Victorian naturalist, the Reverend William Kirby, tried in the 1850s:

> In this strange and apparently cruel operation one circumstance is truly remarkable. The larva of the Ichneumon, through every day, perhaps for months, gnaws the inside of the caterpillar, and though at last it has devoured almost every part of it except the skin and intestines, carefully all this time it avoids injuring the vital organs, as if aware that its own existence depends on that of the insect upon which it preys! . . . What would be the impression which a similar instance amongst the race of quadrupeds would make upon us? If, for example, an animal . . . should be found to feed upon the inside of a dog, devouring only those parts not essential to life, while it cautiously left uninjured the heart, arteries, lungs, and intestines, — should we not regard such an instance as a perfect prodigy, as an example of instinctive forbearance almost miraculous?[5]

In addition to the larvae's admirable efficiency, Kirby also found praise for the mother wasp's care and industry in picking a suitable victim for the benefit of progeny she would never see (since wasps do not rear their young); if only all mothers showed such devotion![6]

Such acrobatic attempts to find harmony and rectitude in a nature that is often as cruel as kind are still very much with us. A recent essay on the praying mantis in *National Geographic* included a horrifying pictorial of the cannibalistic copulation for which mantids are famous. The captions to those photographs concluded with an attempt to end on a virtuous note of fatherly love:

> [First photo] Sensing the female's pheromones, a Chinese mantis approaches stealthily, then makes a sudden flying leap onto her back. [Second photo] As mating proceeds, the female clutches the male around the

neck and begins to feed on his head. [Final photo] Though now decapitated, the male has a nervous system that enables him to continue mating, sometimes for hours. Looking on the bright side, some scientists have suggested that the male benefits his offspring by providing protein for the female during egg production.[7]

Jokes aside, I would rather not even imagine what kind of naturalistic ethics could be derived from such phenomena.

The naive search for morals in nature is also surprisingly evident among academics; witness the highly publicized embarrassment of the editors of the journal *Social Text* at the hands of physicist Alan Sokal.[8] While the journal's editors have been justly chastised for publishing a paper that they clearly did not understand, they also deserve criticism for falling for Sokal's (farcical) assertion that emerging ideas about physics could have profound political and moral implications; Sokal states in his paper, for example, that chaos theory and certain elements of quantum mechanics are somehow politically liberating, as though our ideas on justice and goodness can hinge in some meaningful way on the determinacy of quantum spin states in subatomic particles.

Though academic in origin, the problems of delineation and value with regard to nature have implications that reach beyond academe. The politics of environmentalism has, I think, greatly suffered in recent years because of this naiveté. As long as matters of environmental policy can be caricatured as a contest between the interests of humans versus the interests of some aspect of an ill-defined "nature" — like spotted owls or snail darters — then it must come as no surprise when many people decide to take the side of the humans. Instead environmentalists should openly admit what we all know to be true: rather than speaking for "nature" (which requires neither spokespersons nor defenders), they are speaking for the interests of people who have certain political or moral judgments about how to use or protect natural resources. Like all other kinds of political debates, environmental politics entails conflicts between the interests of people, not between the interests of nature on the one hand and people on the other.

Nature has no morals, nature has no politics; consequently nature has no interests. Environmentalists cannot speak for nature because nature has nothing to say. Protecting endangered species, keeping our environments habitable, pleasant, and biologically diverse — these are all still good things, but not because they are good for nature; nature will continue to exist with or without us, and with no regard to our actions or inactions. Being environmentally conscientious is good because it is good for *us;* it is a form of enlightened self-interest.

PROBLEMS FOR HUMAN NATURE

Similar problems of delineation and value exist for human nature. Since the boundaries of nature are problematic (and, ironically, artificial), we're left with only the fuzziest outline of *human* nature (presumably universal human traits that stem from nature itself). As with nature in general, it is useful to consider human nature's opposite: What aspect of human behavior does human nature leave out?

It seems to me that the only consistent and coherent definition of human nature is the one identified by Dan Flores in this volume. Human nature is that set of characteristics that are truly universal by virtue of their biological foundation. Peoples may differ vastly from one another culturally or socially, but our biological, genetic distinctions are comparatively trivial. It would be proper to regard those human traits that are biologically determined as constituting human nature.

But what does this leave us? Again, the history of science is not particularly encouraging; biological determinism has an extremely sullied record. Many times and in many places behavioral traits were chalked up to human nature for clearly political reasons — usually to lay a "scientific" foundation for discrimination against particular racial or ethnic groups.[9] But these were generally cases in which scientists were deliberately trying to draw distinctions between the natures of different groups of people. The more recent incarnation of biological determinism — particularly sociobiology — overtly tries to identify traits that are universal to all people.

While this is an important distinction, I do not think that it will leave much room for useful or interesting discoveries. Biological determinism, a rather crude analytical tool, will probably yield only crude knowledge. For biological reasons, humans need to sleep on a roughly daily basis and for significant periods of time. For biological reasons, humans do not breathe water. For biological reasons, humans cannot fly under their own power. There are many such biological influences on behavior, but I doubt that historians would find many of them compelling.

The truly interesting elements of human behavior — like aggression, xenophobia, creativity, or compassion — are all much more complex than the simple traits mentioned above and are therefore much harder to trace back to any clear biological foundation. Once again there is an enormous problem of definition. Probably the greatest scientific effort in this regard has gone toward trying to determine the biological bases of human intelligence. While an enormous amount of fascinating work has been done, almost no one in the field today still believes that intelligence is a single, well-defined entity, capable of unambiguous measurement; more likely, what we refer to as intelligence is a complex network of traits, activities, and capabilities. Obviously if the trait itself cannot be defined clearly, the hopes of finding a clear biological basis for it evaporate.

But perhaps all this still misses the point. As with broader nature, our perceptions of human nature come up against a problem of value. Even if we do find biological bases for interesting human traits — a real delineation of human nature — what does this really get us? Even if humans really are violent, or altruistic, or acquisitive *by nature,* so what? I happen to agree with Dan Flores that sociobiological investigations may tell us as much as we have to learn about human nature. But I do not think that this will be very much.

If, for example, complex traits and behaviors are shaped, even profoundly, by the dynamics of selfish genes, this revelation will hardly mean that we are blindly and eternally doomed to play out the whims of our genotypic puppet masters. For example, I have a pet theory (as far as I know, totally unsubstantiated by rigorous investigation) that provides a biologically deterministic insight into the universal lament that everything that tastes good is bad for us. My theory focuses on those foods that are rich in fat (as are most of my favorites). For the vast majority of the duration of human existence, the greatest threats to life were starvation and exposure. Consequently prehistoric humans could have increased their individual chances for survival by eating large amounts of animal fat, which provides the body with good insulation and long-lasting stores of energy. It seems quite plausible to me that our distant ancestors may have, in fact, evolved a naturally selected, genetic predisposition to want to eat fatty foods. Those humans with the "fat-loving" gene or genes had a slightly greater probability of surviving long enough to reproduce, and the genotype survived. Today, at least in those parts of the world where I hear the lament about fatty food, starvation and exposure have been vastly reduced as threats to human survival; because we live so much longer than our distant ancestors, we worry instead about heart disease and atherosclerosis — conditions very much worsened by large intakes of fat. Saddled with these ancient genes, we find that our favorite foods are no longer good for us.[10]

I like this theory. I find it economical, powerful, and compelling. But of course, I can take no solace in it. Eating a lot of fat is still bad for me, and my arteries will not forgive me should I choose to pound down a box of Snickers just because my genes entice me to do so.

No less a sociobiologist than E. O. Wilson has recognized that such biological influences do not constitute an iron determinism. In his conclusion to *On Human Nature,* Wilson argued that any knowledge we glean from sociobiology will still leave us with moral and political choices:

> Human nature is not just the array of outcomes attained in existing societies. It is also the potential array that might be achieved through conscious design by future societies. By looking over the realized social systems of hundreds of animal species and deriving the principles by which these systems have evolved, we can be certain that all human choices represent only a tiny subset of those theoretically possible.[11]

Violence or compassion may be in our nature, but we can still choose to cultivate certain elements of that nature and discourage others.

Which traits we choose to encourage or restrain must obviously be matters of political and cultural judgment. The very existence of these trends in human behavior cannot bestow any moral value to them. Their places in human nature (if such exist) obliges us only to contend, not comply, with them.

Why do we have this power of choice over biological determinism (while the ants and wasps generally do not)? The answer almost certainly lies in that same device that gives us these elaborate traits to begin with: our large and complex brains. Ironically, an appreciation of the ability of humans to transcend rigid determinism can come from an unlikely source: the history of machines.

HARDWIRED FOR FLEXIBILITY

Nothing looks more inflexible and deterministic than a machine: springs coil, wires pull, gears mesh, all in lockstep mechanism. As machines grew more complex, they left less and less room for flexibility or adaptation; while a pulley or a rack and pinion were extremely versatile devices (they could perform numerous functions in different environments), an electric can opener can really do only one thing.

This trend toward increasingly narrow-purpose machines, however, has been stunningly and unexpectedly punctuated by the development of a nearly universal machine: the electronic digital computer.[12] Although virtually every one of this technology's creators expected computers to be little more than very fast and powerful calculators, computers have become much more. In writing these words, for example, I am currently using one of these machines for a task that its original designers never imagined — a task, in fact, that this machine was *not* technically designed to perform. The hardware in my computer knows nothing about word processing, nor about the thousands of other purposes for which people use computers — drawing, designing, scheduling, communicating, playing, and so on. Yet the machine is able to perform all of these tasks, and undoubtedly many more yet unimagined. In this sense, computers are universal machines; they can do anything that humans can figure out how to tell them to do.

Yet they are machines. They are hardwired collections of mechanical parts. The central unit of the computer does nothing more than control the flow of electrons through a straightforward (though intricate) set of electronic switches. But by controlling the sequences in which the electrons flow through these circuits, it is possible to give rise to different kinds of actions, different kinds of behavior. With a simple change in software instructions, the same machine that was one moment serving as a versatile typewriter can the next moment be displaying artwork, playing music, or simulating flight. Computers are hardwired, but they are deliberately hardwired to be flexible — to do different things in different environments. By increasing the complexity of the networks of electronic switches in a computer's "brain," we can increase the ease and versatility by which computers learn new behaviors.

Computer hardware may be extremely flexible by machine standards, but it is clunky and rigid beyond comparison next to the stupifyingly complex "wetware" that resides inside the human skull.[13] Out of hardware that is immeasurably complex, software that virtually writes itself, and interactions between the two that are likely to remain intractable for some time to come in spite of scientists' ingenious efforts to the contrary, arise human traits and behaviors that are complex and flexible beyond the fantasies of human engineers.

It may turn out, as sociobiologists suggest, that our genes have hardwired us for certain behaviors, for a particular human nature. Our genes may have endowed us with aggression or altruism to maximize our (and their) chances for survival in dangerous environments. But the most successful survival trait of all is *flexibility* — the ability to adapt to changing environments — and the human brain is hardwired for it. The same piece of hardware that allows us to study human nature allows us to defy it when we wish.

CONCLUSION

In spite of the problems of delineation and value, I do not expect to see appeals to nature or human nature vanish anytime soon; the essentially romantic visions of nature and morality are probably too deeply rooted in many cultures. But I think that it is important for historians to recognize that the problems associated with these terms preclude their use as actors in historical narratives. Actors in stories must be well-defined entities with will and agency. Nature is far too poorly defined and totally lacking in will to serve this purpose. Human nature, although becoming better defined, will never have the potency to constrain, much less rival, the role of human choice in history.

NOTES

1. Excellent discussions of the gender dimensions of visions of nature can be found in the works of Evelyn Fox Keller, Carolyn Merchant, and Londa L. Schiebinger.

2. Bill Cronon has hinted at this problem in his recent essay, "The Trouble with Wilderness; or, Getting Back to the Wrong Nature," in *Uncommon Ground: Toward Reinventing Nature,* ed. William Cronon (New York: Norton, 1995), 69–90. In that essay, Cronon exquisitely historicizes *wilderness* and explores the difficulties of its use as a category of analysis. I am suggesting here that what is true for *wilderness* is equally true for *nature.*

3. Robert Proctor has examined the moral appeal to nature and its role in Nazi genocide in *Racial Hygiene: Medicine under the Nazis* (Cambridge: Harvard University Press, 1988).

4. Stephen Jay Gould, *Hen's Teeth and Horse's Toes* (New York: Norton, 1983), 33–35.

5. Ibid., p. 40.

6. Ibid., p. 39.

7. Edward S. Ross, "Mantids: The Praying Predators," *National Geographic,* 165, no. 2 (February 1984): 274. The gender dimension to this narrative is obvious; one could create a completely different, but equally absurd, anthropomorphized story by focusing on how the copulation begins (with the male's surprise attack) and conclude that he gets precisely what he deserves. In fairness to Ross, it should be noted that the *text* (rather than caption) notes that once copulation has commenced, the male's job is done and he is now good for little more than food anyway.

8. Sokal submitted a satirical article, "Transgressing the Boundaries: Toward a Transformative Hermeneutics of Quantum Gravity," purporting to examine the postmodern character of modern physics via a jargon-filled but nonsensical string of unexamined assertions and quotations from Derrida and Lacan. The editors of *Social Text* published the article as genuine in its spring/summer 1996 issue. When Sokal went public with the hoax, the ensuing storm of dispute eventually reached the pages of *Newsweek* and *The New York Times.* See Alan Sokal, "A Physicist Experiments with Cultural Studies," *Lingua Franca* 6, no. 4 (May/June 1996): 62–64; the ensuing roundtable discussion, "Mystery Science Theater," *Lingua France* 6, no. 5 (July/August 1996): 54–64; and Steven Weinberg, "Sokal's Hoax," *New York Review of Books* 43, no. 13, 8 August 1996, 11–15.

9. In addition to Proctor's *Racial Hygiene,* see Stephen Jay Gould's *The Mismeasure of Man* (New York: Norton, 1981).

10. I have yet to see any rigorous test of this hypothesis. Researchers at Rockefeller

University, however, believe they have identified a biochemical basis for craving dietary fat (though in rats) — a brain protein called galanin. This research group also believes that the production of galanin is regulated genetically rather than environmentally. See Carol Ezzell, "Craving Fat? Blame it on a Brain Protein," *Science News* 142, no. 19, 7 November 1992, 311.

11. Edward O. Wilson, *On Human Nature* (New York: Bantam, 1978), p. 203.

12. See Paul Ceruzzi, "An Unforeseen Revolution: Computers and Expectations, 1935–1985," in *Imagining Tomorrow: History, Technology, and the American Future,* ed. Joseph J. Corn (Cambridge: MIT Press, 1986), 188–201.

13. It is impossible to provide meaningful comparisons of the "computing power" between conventional computers and human brains. Their network architectures are very different and they use different kinds of switches, and it is becoming increasingly clear in any case that the behavior of organic brains arises from layers of complexity that reach far beyond the raw number of switches or their connections. It is illustrative to note that it requires large conglomerations of conventional computer circuitry to mimic even minuscule portions of organic brains in so-called neural nets.

CONTRIBUTORS

William deBuys holds a Ph.D. in American studies from the University of Texas at Austin. He is an environmental scholar and activist who works in Santa Fe, New Mexico. DeBuys is the author of several landmark studies in environmental history, including *River of Traps, Enchantment and Exploitation: The Life and Hard Times of a New Mexico Mountain Range,* and the forthcoming *Salt Dreams.*

Dan Flores received his Ph.D. from Texas A&M University and taught at Texas Tech before becoming the A. B. Hammond Chair of History at the University of Montana. His books include *Caprock Canyonlands: Journeys into the Heart of the Southern Plains* and *Journal of an Indian Trader: Anthony Glass and the Texas Trading Frontier.* Beyond his ongoing research on Native Americans and bison, Flores is currently writing an environmental history of the Rocky Mountains and the greater Southwest.

John Herron is a Ph.D. candidate in western history at the University of New Mexico. Herron is currently completing his dissertation on the significance of nature in American culture. He has authored several essays on gender, science, and environmental ideology, and his current project examines the lives and legacies of noted environmental scientists Clarence King, Bob Marshall, and Rachel Carson.

Paul Hirt teaches western and environmental history at Washington State University. Hirt is active in many environmental history projects, including the development of environmental history teaching resources on the World Wide Web. His book, *A Conspiracy of Optimism: Management of the National Forests Since World War II*, unravels the complex politics and economics of America's most powerful land agency, the Forest Service.

Andrew Kirk is a visiting assistant professor at Syracuse University. He is the author of *The Gentle Science: A History of the Conservation Library* and several articles on western environmentalism. His current research focuses on the appropriate technology movement, radical politics, and the environmental movement.

Vera Norwood, professor of American studies at the University of New Mexico, is a feminist scholar with major research interests in women's studies and responses to nature and the built environment. Norwood has published work on Rachel Carson, Mary Austin, Laura Gilpin, and a wide variety of southwestern women writers and artists. She is the author of several well-known works on the field of environment and culture, including *Made from This Earth: American Women and Nature* and *The Desert Is No Lady*.

Timothy Moy received his A.B. in history and science from Harvard in 1985 and his Ph.D. in history from U.C. Berkeley in 1992. He is currently assistant professor of history, specializing in the history of science and technology, at the University of New Mexico. His research interests focus on the historical relationships between institutional culture and science and technology in the U.S. military during the twentieth century.

Max Oelschlaeger teaches in the philosophy and religious studies department at the University of North Texas. He specializes in the study of environmental ethics, environmental philosophy, and the philosophy of wilderness. Oelschlaeger is the author of *Caring for Creation, The Idea of Wilderness, The Wilderness Condition*, and many articles on the philosophical, moral, and intellectual roots of environmental protection and environmental ethics.

Virginia Scharff is associate professor of history at the University of New Mexico. Her books include *Taking the Wheel: Women and the Coming of the Motor Age, Present Tense: The United States Since World War II, and Coming of Age: The United States Since 1890*. She is currently writing a book about women, mobility, and the history of the American West.